UNDERSTAND YOUR BODY

MULTIDIMENSIONAL HEALING METHOD TO REGAIN YOUR HEALTH

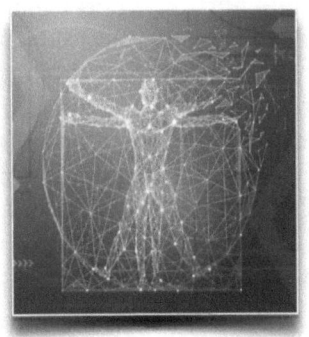

GARY L. STORKAN D.C.

ARNICA PRESS

DISCLAIMER

The material contained in this book has been written for informational purposes and is not intended as a substitute for medical advice, nor is it intended to diagnose, treat, cure, or prevent disease. The author and the publisher disclaim any liability arising directly or indirectly from the use of this book. The author and publisher do not recommend any specific treatment, supplement, medication, dietary implementation or behavioral programs without first consulting your personal physician, healthcare provider, or therapist. If you have a medical issue or illness, consult a qualified physician. Be sure to check with your own qualified health care provider before beginning any protocols or procedures discussed in this book, or before stopping or altering any diet, lifestyle, or other therapies previously recommended to you by your health care provider. The treatments described in this book my have side effects and carry other known and unknown risks. The treatments and protocols described in this book are for reference only and not intended to teach any technique, but rather to encourage further investigation of those techniques. In addition, Lyme disease is a controversial topic and this book should not be seen as the final word regarding Lyme disease medical care. The statements in this book have not been evaluated by the united states FDA. Use of this book is at your own risk.

Published by ARNICA PRESS
www.ArnicaPress.com

Copyright © 2019 Gary L. Storkan DC
www.storkanchiropractic.com

Printed in the United States of America
ISBN : 978-1-7336446-4-8

All rights reserved.
No part of this book may be reproduced or transmitted in any form or by any means, electronic or mechanical, including photocopying, recording, or by any information storage and retrieval system, without the prior written permission from the Publisher.

To my wondrous wife Jennifer

all my invaluable Patients

TABLE OF CONTENTS

INTRODUCTION   11

PART One ~ Know your body

Your Energy Grid	24
Components of your Health	27
Physical components of your health	28
Mental~Emotional components of your health	30
Metabolic components of your health	32
The Reflex Points	34
Your Energy patterns	36
The Circadian Clock	37
The Adrenals	38
Mild adrenal burnout	42
Severe adrenal burnout	43
Coping mechanism	43
Adrenal burnout and chronic fatigue	44
Adrenal fatigue in various age groups	44

Adrenal fatigue and anxiety	45
Your nervous system	45
Occasional stress versus chronic stress	46
Adrenal recovery	46
Remedies	48
The Thyroid	51
The Pituitary	57
Food allergies	59
Parasites	63
Mold	64
Fungus	65
Candida	66
Lyme disease	67
Lyme Treatment Protocol	69

PART 2 ~ Talk to your body

About Dimensions	74
Working with Dimensions	78
Muscle Testing	84
How to Muscle Test	85
Psychological Reversal	89
Polarity Point	92
Switching	93
First Aspect	93
Second Aspect	94

Third Aspect~ Ileocecal Valve test	96
Ileocecal Valve Reset	98
Finding the Priority Organ	103
Working on the Priority Organ	104
Core Beliefs	108
The Harmonization Process	111
Reprograming the Spine	113
My addition for Advanced Reprograming	114
My Protocol Guidelines	115

PART 3 ~ Heal your Body

Self~Testing technique	128
The Ten Golden Rules that I Follow	129
The Five Golden Rules I share with Patients	136
Questionnaire	139
The Universal Presence	144
Final Thoughts	147
References	150
About the Author	153

ACKNOWLEDGMENTS

I wish to express my heartfelt gratitude to all who inspired and guided me on my fascinating journey while gathering extraordinary knowledge and priceless experiences.

I must give credit where credit is due. The primary technique that I use is *Total Body Modification*, developed by Dr. Victor Frank. Without his wonderful mentorship and guidance during my personal study with him, I would not be experiencing the success that I am today. I am very grateful for his genius.

I am also thankful to one of his colleagues, Dr. John Thie, who developed the *Touch for Health foundation*, where I learned the art of muscle testing. I thank Dr. Dick Versendaal, with whom I didn't spend a lot of time with, but gained a few techniques that I still use to this day. As far as evaluating the spine, my experience with Dr. L. John Faye and Dr. Henry Gillet, their *Motion Palpation* work has been invaluable.

On the emotional front Dr. James V. Durlacher gave me a very important tool called *Acupower*. Over the last thirty years I have found this technique to absolutely change people's lives.

The newest work that I must give credit to is *Core Beliefs* by Dr. Kevin S. Millet, the new owner and director of TBM. I've also found this work significant in the short term that I have used it.

Finally, I would like to thank Sabrina Mesko for her support and faith in helping me realize this book. My gratitude for her help in creating this book is unlimited.

Last but not least, I wish to thank my patients. I am so grateful to them for allowing me to work and learn from them, often more than from the many seminars I've attended. In fact, it is through an unusual experience with one of my patients that I learned the unique concept, upon which this book is focused.

Life works in wondrous ways if we are receptive and remain open for a miracle. I thank you all and am thrilled to share all my gained knowledge with you, my dear reader.

May you find answers for what you are seeking, and may they help you enjoy a life of lasting health and precious happiness.

Introduction

The book that you hold in your hands is a unique navigation map to help you understand your most precious and valuable possession - your body. This vault of fascinating information that I am about to open and share with you, is meant to guide you to your optimal state of health, so you can get back the life you deserve and want.

The fact is, nobody feels your body as well as you do. Nobody lives in it but you. Therefore nobody can understand it as well as you can. Once you truly tune-in and learn to translate your body's message, you will gain the key to maintaining your optimum health.

I see the body as a miracle that will do whatever it needs to survive. I mean, when you consider the toxicity in our environment! My God, we all should be dead, if our bodies could not adapt! Your body sends you messages all the time, even at this very moment. It may be hungry, tired, cold, in pain, or in need of special care. It may have discomforts, aches, and persistent ailments that you may have accepted as your new normal state.

Sometimes these messages are small, other times desperate and alarming. When a message has been ignored, dismissed or neglected, the body will stoically attempt to heal itself. But if it can't manage to conquer the challenge on its own, it will continue to communicate with you and urge you to pay attention. The calls will escalate until you feel increased discomfort and finally take notice.

Are you aware and paying attention?
My philosophy is that the body is an integrated unit of energy, and that because of certain powerful triggers that occur throughout our lives, the body has to continuously use its precious energy to address these triggers in order to stay balanced.
The triggers are like invisible disturbing activators that agitate the body's healthy natural energy frequency and prevent it from functioning properly.

I have worked with patients over three decades and my focus has always been to find as many of these triggers as I can, and help relieve them from the body. The body can then use its energy to maintain the balance that it was designed to do. This may sound simple, but it is a demanding and intricate process.

Triggers are complex, well hidden, and shrewdly disguised. There may be a multitude of them, for there is rarely just one simple isolated trigger. They cause the human subtle energy field to lose is healthy rhythm and veer off balance. Hence, a dysfunction occurs that affects the entire field of your delicate inner harmony. The trickle down effect reverberates and spreads to other regions of your body, further disguising the true culprit. The longer this goes on, the more labyrinthine it becomes.

Finding the trigger requires tenacious subtle energy detective work. Careful discernment is needed to decipher every nuance that is being communicated through the body's responses to various triggering discomforts.

The body wants to communicate, and does so all the time. You may be listening, paying attention, and recognizing that something is off balance, but do you actually understand the message?

My whole focus through the healing process is to talk to the body and find out what are the unseen triggers that are causing this dysfunction. What is provoking the body to have to spend so much energy dealing with all these challenges caused by the outside triggers?

They could be anything from food and allergies, unresolved emotions, pollen, a wide array of unique factors that are limiting the body from doing what it needs to do in order to stay in perfect balance, or as good a balance as it can.

There are many nuances to my work which includes a complex array of various advanced and quite extraordinary healing modalities, that I have perfected specifically for the purpose of deep communication with the body to alleviate its discomforts and imbalances.

In this book, I will reveal my healing protocol that is a culmination of over three decades of dedicated work

with my countless patients from all corners of the world. They are always the greatest teachers.
Each case is unique and carries treasured information that can open another door of possibility to find the greatest gift in this world - a key to vibrant and everlasting health.

Through the many years of practice, my patients often asked if I intend to write a book and reveal my fascinating discoveries. Well, finally the moment has come. I am excited and eager to share my golden nuggets of helpful knowledge with all who seek to decipher the hidden language of their bodies and long to get back their life.

How did I get on this path of such unique purpose and aim?
All my life has been filled with divine intervention that has guided me through this exciting and unpredictable process.

I was born in Hastings, Michigan and enjoyed a happy childhood as a free spirited child. At an early age I got into music, played the trumpet and became quite good at it.
My father who worked seven days a week, taught me good principles to live by, and my mother was an excellent pianist who played the violin with close to perfect pitch. I can still hear her melodic voice from the kitchen, interrupting my trumpet practice while urging me to improve:
"That should have been an F sharp!"
Despite my naturally eccentric nature, they lovingly

supported my music, so I became a student conductor for the high school band. I was always kind of unusual or even a bit odd. Instead of the customary baseball cap, I wore a beret, just to assert my strong tendency for originality. One could say I always did things in a lot of ways a bit differently that other people.

I was first chair of the high school band most of the time that I was there, and then I went to Western Michigan University and graduated with a degree in teaching music.

Naturally, one would expect that I would spend my life behind the piano or playing any other instrument, teaching and organizing school concerts, but obviously the Universe had a different plan for me.

I was going through an adventurous period in my early life, when I got into a VW bus with my girlfriend at the time, and spent almost an entire year on the road, traveling across the country. The final destination was the East Coast, which is where her parents were located. So we travelled all the way from the wild West and finally ended up staying on Cape Cod for about six months. I worked as an occasional temporary carpenter during the time out there.

We were practicing yoga on a regular basis and as fate would have it, I hurt my back while pushing myself too hard into a yoga posture. Ironically, something that was meant to help, actually caused me physical discomfort and became a life changing event.

The Universe has a funny way of pushing us in directions of our destiny. So in order to recover from my injury, I went to see a chiropractor out there, who did muscle testing on me, and my world changed in an instant.

I was so intrigued by this approach, that just as soon as we returned to California, I joined the Touch for Health foundation. I became an instructor and learned how to teach this technique, which is a laymen's muscle testing program. I was very involved with them and fascinated with the transformative work.

And as fate would have it, one day while working at the foundation, a lady appeared and asked me a life altering question:
"We need somebody to work in our chiropractic office. Would you be wiling to do that?"
And I thought, boy, this is my chance to really use this stuff in clinical setting!
I jumped at the opportunity and said without hesitation: "Yes, absolutely!"

So my life took another unexpected turn as I moved to San Francisco and worked for Dr. Frank Young for a few years. I saw him do some phenomenal things with chiropractic, while I worked in his clinic doing kinesiology and nutritional counseling on patients. I witnessed how he performed miracles using the chiropractic technique, but what really intrigued me, was how powerful this approach was for getting people out of pain and working with them from that standpoint.

As a predictable next step, I decided to go to the chiropractic school, get a license, and follow my calling to work with people on my own.

While there, I naturally got involved in the muscle skeletal aspects of healing, but still used the kinesiology as well. Soon thereafter, I got into my own practice, and the two modalities just kind of blended together. The rest as they say, is history.

What fascinated me right from the beginning was a combination of things. I always had this idea that the body was integrated and that you could not just separate the spine without looking at how the organs were functioning, as well as the delicate emotional state somebody was in. I observed that a bit while practicing kinesiology in Dr. Young's office, and noticed that he did nothing as far as acknowledging any emotions or addressing any of the complex metabolic aspects.

I really noticed a connection there between what he was working with, and what I was seeing in that office. So when I launched my own practice, I pretty much stayed almost conclusively with the muscle skeletal approach, because that was basically my background and where I wanted to get my practice started. But after only a couple of years, my work just

morphed with my whole philosophy.
And from that point on, it was just a matter of finding techniques that supported my all-inclusive philosophy.

So I embarked on an enthusiastic search, attended numerous fascinating seminars, and was fortunate to learn powerful techniques directly and in-person from various pioneers in the field.

I would then carefully select out of those techniques certain aspects that I found most effective and supportive of my philosophy. I am happy to say, that I still use them to this day.

The next decisive turning point that inspired me to expand my work into a more esoteric direction occurred about three years into my practice.
After a regular visit at my office, one of my patients exclaimed:
" You need to learn this TBM (Total Body Modification) technique, so I don't have to keep going to Denver to get it done, to handle all of my allergies!"
I thought that this sounded rather compelling.

A fascinating synergy followed. Just as soon as I put this idea of exploring the mentioned technique into the Universe, that is precisely what happened!

All of a sudden, I began receiving flyers in the mail, about exactly this technique. The more I read about it, the more I was interested. But all the seminars were long studies, and quite a distance away.

Until one day, I received a notice about a weekend morning seminar in Albuquerque.
And I thought: "How perfect is that!"

So I studied in the mornings and worked on my patients the same day later in the afternoon, immediately trying out the technique. It was an exciting study, full of captivating information. It was at this time that I learned the desensitizing part of the technique that I still use today. Every time I used it on a person, they came back to me with enthusiasm and gratitude:
"I don't know what you did, but I don't have allergies any more."

Naturally, I began using it more and as a result witnessed true miracles. Now, this is a major part of my practice as I see about 90 % of my patients improve and literally get their lives back.

With time, I discovered another crucial element in the effectiveness of communicating with the body. This established my unique approach that offered a decisive difference in the effectiveness of my work. From a viewpoint that all matter including the human body is vibration, I began paying attention to the subtle frequency energy field of my patients. I quickly came upon the crucial question; how can one communicate with the physical body, if in a desperate attempt of self-preservation, the body literally sort of "escapes" into a different dimension? It may be quite impossible to establish a line of communication with the body that is functioning on an entirely different frequency field, in an attempt to find shelter and protect itself from the threatening upheaval of the here and now.

We know, that simply in order to survive, it is not unusual for one to take refuge from the present situation through profound emotional detachment. If one escapes with their mind to a faraway land, what makes us think the physical body's frequency can't do the same? In fact it can.

Later in the book I will reveal my extraordinary odyssey of how I discovered and established the groundbreaking intra-dimensional connection with the physical body, when it shifts its natural frequency of being in the present, into a distant frequency that is almost unreachable.

In an attempt for self-preservation, which is a mechanism most often triggered by pain or fear, many of us escape into a different frequency field, where we seek distance from the source of trauma. We subconsciously isolate ourselves, and often remain stuck and out of touch with the reality of our current state.

Clearly, if you wish to help promote the healing process of the body, you must be talking to it on the same wavelength. Otherwise, it's like a scrambled radio signal that no one can decode.
In this book, I will reveal how I came upon this technique, and developed a system to undo this condition. This has become my signature discovery

that magnifies the effectiveness of all other energy healing techniques and modalities.

It is a unique subtle frequency procedure that extends its reach beyond our usual, often limited perception. The body is simply incredible in its ability of adapting to different situations and various toxins. And granted, we have a high disease rate and chronic diseases that are killing people. But I think that generally speaking, our bodies are miraculous, the way they can acclimate to the toxicity and emotional challenges that go on in our lives.

But it robs the person of their full fulfillment of life, and that is precisely what I am focused on preventing and eliminating. When our bodies have to deal with these immense ongoing obstacles, they can't fully enjoy and experience life, because they are spending too much energy just adapting. My whole goal is to give someone their life back, so they don't have to constantly worry and deal with continuous body dysfunction and pain.

I am thrilled to share with you this compelling discovery, and hope you'll find this book a most beneficial tool, to help you reclaim what you so rightfully deserve… a state of optimal health, happiness and abundance of the Spirit.
Let the words on these pages serve as a catalyst in reclaiming your optimum life.

DR. Gary

I.
Know Your Body

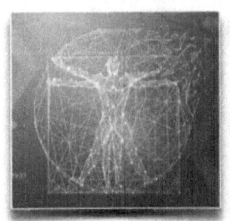

Your Energy Grid

All of your bodily systems are intricately interconnected. I see the human body as a big, complex and incredibly resilient energy grid. Nonetheless it is also quite sensitive to any kind of outside stimuli, harmonious as well as disruptive.
As an example how this kind of a grid operates, let's say you hung it up and taped down the corners of it, with a fair amount of tension in that grid.

If you take any part of that grid, the top, corner, side, or the bottom, and pull on it, you will create a distortion. As a result, even the smallest disturbance is going to warp and deform every single other part of that grid. Anything that happens to it, like an injury, an organ dysfunction, let's say food allergies, or any emotional triggers that occur, they will affect and distort all other aspects of the body.

In my opinion, this is why the body cannot perform in balanced health. It has to expend so much energy while correcting itself, and taking care of that distortion. As a result, it simply cannot spend the energy on basic and regular function of a normal life.

This is the meaning of my ongoing pursuit to *give someone their life back*. I focus on taking away these unwanted distortions, and therefore allow the body to function as a homeostatic grid, maintaining homeostasis and normal balance.

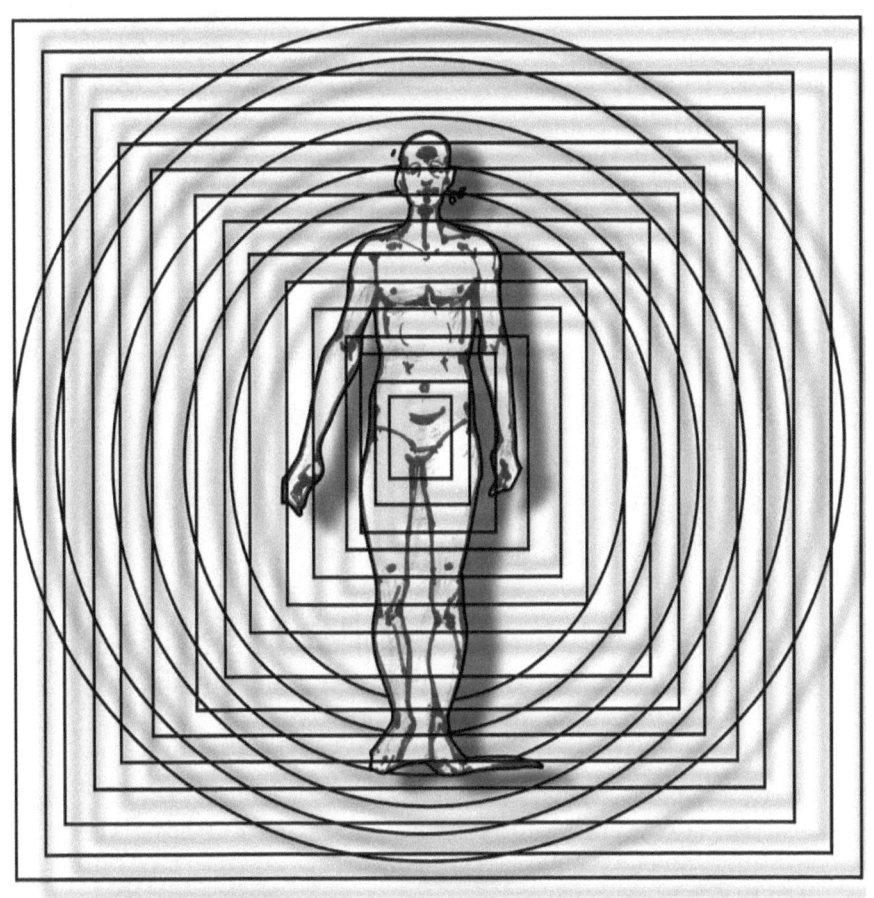

YOUR OPTIMAL HEALTHY SUBTLE ENERGY GRID

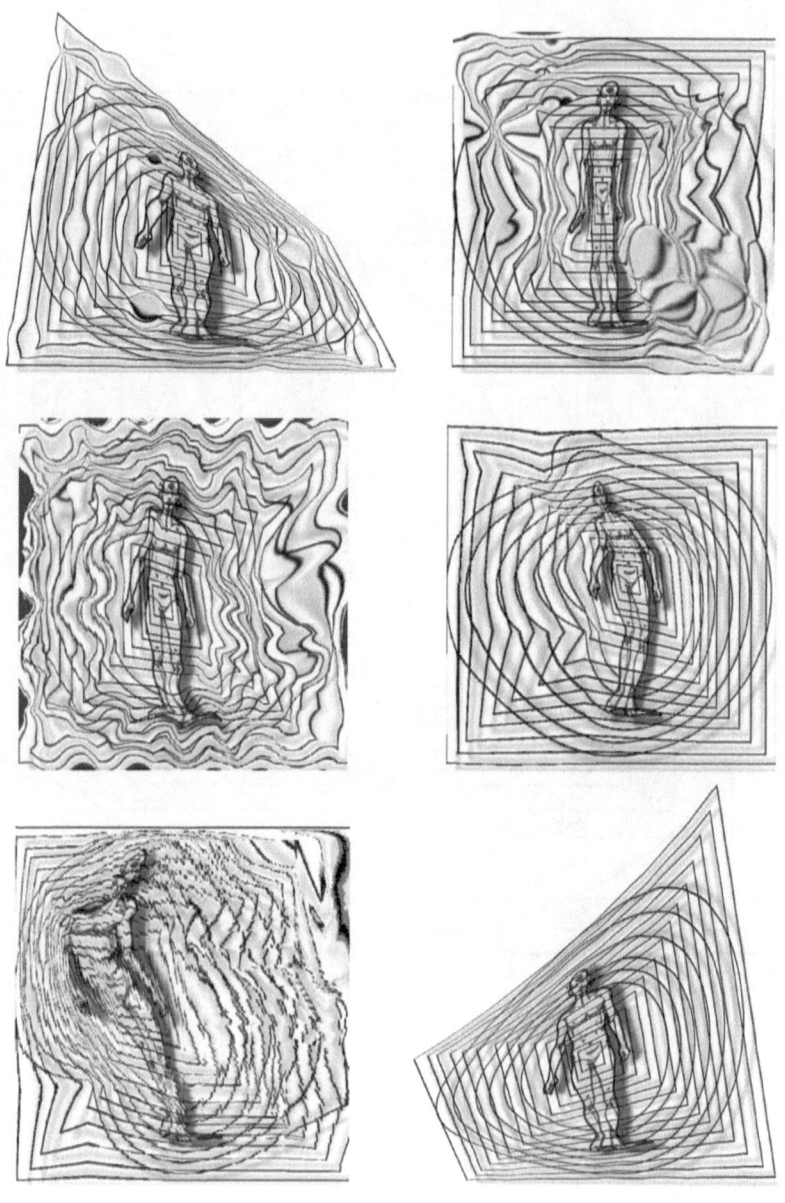

UNHEALTHY SUBTLE ENERGY GRID DISTORTIONS

The Components of your Health

My philosophy has always been that there is a mental-emotional component, a metabolic component, and a physical or muscle-skeletal component to health. This represents the basic triangle with which a lot of health practitioners work.

I've taken this concept a little bit further and have discovered ways of working with each one of these areas very specifically and in greater detail. When various challenges come up, I can address them in a very precise way, rather than just generally assuming and categorizing:
"This looks like a mental and emotional issue, and you need counseling."

I have found techniques that actually work with those situations on a very direct basis, so that I can remedy them immediately, and not wait for a lengthy process of the patient struggling through twenty years of counseling.

People most often come to see me because they have some kind of organ dysfunction, and have been seeking help from a few doctors, but unfortunately nobody seemed to know what to do with them.
As a Doctor of Chiropractic, I include spinal manipulation in my therapy, but my passion and expertise lies in deep metabolic work, which entails careful, detail oriented exploration of various organ diseases and chronic organ dysfunctions.

The Physical Components of your Health

Because of my chiropractic background, I consider the spine a most important component of overall skeletal health. Its marvelous mechanical function and how it influences the neurological input or output to the spine and the rest of the body is truly miraculous. What is likewise fascinating and quite astounding, is the way it restricts neurological input throughout the body, as a direct result of its lack of function. I pay much attention to hidden muscle dysfunction, trigger points and tensions that can be just as influential as the spine. I find that when a person suffers an injury, it also affects the metabolic function of their body, conceals organ dysfunction and disturbs their overall emotional function.

In a case of a car accident, there may be a significant consequential emotional component as well, such as a deep-set fear that formed during the accident. If the injury occurred from a fall, the person may carry unresolved anger, persistent fear, or another hidden emotional component that is associated with that injury as well. That's where I tie everything together. When a new patient seeks my help with a problem in their lower back, I certainly look at the skeletal and muscular components, but I also have to consider the liver and other possible organ dysfunctions as well as any emotional issues that may play a contributing role. I look at all variables of the full, whole picture.

VERTEBRAL COLUMN AND CORRESPONDING ORGANS

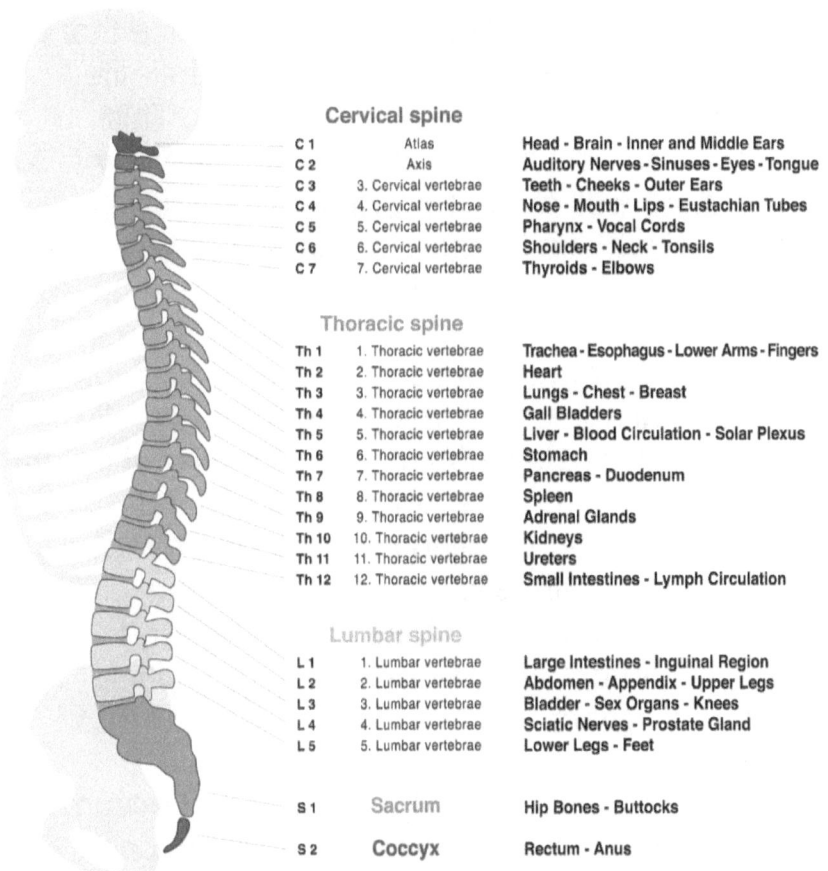

Cervical spine

C 1	Atlas	Head - Brain - Inner and Middle Ears
C 2	Axis	Auditory Nerves - Sinuses - Eyes - Tongue
C 3	3. Cervical vertebrae	Teeth - Cheeks - Outer Ears
C 4	4. Cervical vertebrae	Nose - Mouth - Lips - Eustachian Tubes
C 5	5. Cervical vertebrae	Pharynx - Vocal Cords
C 6	6. Cervical vertebrae	Shoulders - Neck - Tonsils
C 7	7. Cervical vertebrae	Thyroids - Elbows

Thoracic spine

Th 1	1. Thoracic vertebrae	Trachea - Esophagus - Lower Arms - Fingers
Th 2	2. Thoracic vertebrae	Heart
Th 3	3. Thoracic vertebrae	Lungs - Chest - Breast
Th 4	4. Thoracic vertebrae	Gall Bladders
Th 5	5. Thoracic vertebrae	Liver - Blood Circulation - Solar Plexus
Th 6	6. Thoracic vertebrae	Stomach
Th 7	7. Thoracic vertebrae	Pancreas - Duodenum
Th 8	8. Thoracic vertebrae	Spleen
Th 9	9. Thoracic vertebrae	Adrenal Glands
Th 10	10. Thoracic vertebrae	Kidneys
Th 11	11. Thoracic vertebrae	Ureters
Th 12	12. Thoracic vertebrae	Small Intestines - Lymph Circulation

Lumbar spine

L 1	1. Lumbar vertebrae	Large Intestines - Inguinal Region
L 2	2. Lumbar vertebrae	Abdomen - Appendix - Upper Legs
L 3	3. Lumbar vertebrae	Bladder - Sex Organs - Knees
L 4	4. Lumbar vertebrae	Sciatic Nerves - Prostate Gland
L 5	5. Lumbar vertebrae	Lower Legs - Feet
S 1	Sacrum	Hip Bones - Buttocks
S 2	Coccyx	Rectum - Anus

Looking at the body from a holistic viewpoint, every component of the spine is in direct and close interaction with organs, our metabolic systems and likewise affects the delicate nuances of our emotional states.

The Mental~ Emotional Components of your Health

Usually a deep-seated emotional experience that a person experienced at a certain time of their life, contributes to their overall state of health. This challenge can occur through ongoing everyday stressors, as well as what I call *a psychological reversal*, which is a bit more serious than just casual stressors.

When I discover an organ dysfunction that involves also a mental and emotional component, I really consider such a combination a most powerful irritant. Usually it stems from the person's childhood. Through the muscle testing process where the patient's body often tells me that there is an emotional component such as anger or fear, I frequently find that the person has endured it for the last 30 or 40 years.

In other words, the emotional triggers that occurred as a result of a challenging family situation or dynamic that one experienced as a child, can leave a persistent and disturbing residue. A powerful energetic pattern gets established in the body, and because it is an actual force of energy, it has to express itself.

It may not do so in the exact same way as it was initially registered and absorbed, but it will definitely express itself in a very similar manner, and will effectively construct a person's life. Let's say that someone had a father who had a very domineering nature and caused a lot of stress in the child's life, by making them feel incompetent or unworthy. That problematic feeling will accompany the child and later adult person through their entire life. They will basically gage the remainder of their life around that feeling that will represent their "normal" expected communication, response and emotional interaction with every person and situation they encounter.

We call it a core belief or a basic perception. That long ago established feeling will construct and affect a persons entire life, capacity for self-evaluation, and will set invisible standards of behavior and nature of communication with others. Their perception of reality will function under the restrictions of that negative belief pattern.

When I work with a person, I have to uncover that feeling. This is a sensitive and complex process. I have to help them open up and recognize their self-imposed limitations that were created long ago as an existential defense mechanism. Once they recognize the source of this restricted belief system, the healing process begins. The system I use is called Acupower developed by Dr. James Durlacher.

The Metabolic Components of your Health

The metabolic components that contribute to your overall health are the various possible organ dysfunctions. As I mentioned, my patients seek me out because they have some kind of organ dysfunction and have not experienced a successful healing process with various doctors they sought. It seems that nobody knows how to help them or what to do with them.

When they finally land in my office, I proceed through all the necessary muscle testing steps, examining all the reflexes for each different organ and gland, and if the muscle comes up weak, it clearly indicates that reflex is off.

I continue through the process and determine which components are showing up as dysfunctional. This differs from the usual approach of practitioners that perhaps don't use the techniques I do.
They usually announce:" All right, I see challenges with liver, adrenals, small and large intestine...", and suggest $500 worth of nutritional supplements to help with these organs and glands.

My approach is different. I seek out the one priority that causes all other body dysfunctions. After finding the one or perhaps a few challenged organs, I guide the patient through "therapy localization process", which I describe in the following case study.

CASE STUDY

Recently a client came to me who was in the sixth dimension, psychologically reversed, and really scrambled in her energy. She suffered from severe migraine headaches, which could oftentimes indicate a liver dysfunction through toxicity, possible adrenal dysfunction, or it could be an indication of physical problem of her neck. I found liver, adrenals, small intestine and large intestine that played a strong role in her overall state.

I had her place her hand on the liver reflex point, and the response came up weak. When I then put my fingers on the adrenal reflex, her muscles just locked in. I asked her if she felt that muscle lock. She confirmed. I explained to her that this is her body saying that the adrenals are affecting her liver. Next, she placed her hand on the small intestine reflex and the same happened, the adrenals were affecting her small intestine as well. The same happened with large intestine reflex. I worked on her adrenals and found that food additives were affecting her adrenals. I harmonized her to the food additives, then returned to check all her organs, liver, the small intestine and large intestine, as well as the adrenals, and all of the reflexes were now negative.

I didn't have to adapt anything else. All I did was address the adrenals, and everything else equalized. The adrenals can cause severe headaches when dysfunctional along with the liver. Her headaches subsided, and she experienced an overall major improvement.

The Reflex Points

Most of the reflexes I use are from the TBM (Total Body Modification) technique. In the treatment session, I usually proceed though those reflexes.

There are also a few additional reflexes that I use which I learned from Dr. Verstendaal and are called the CRA (contact reflex analysis) technique.

I know there are other therapeutic systems that have developed their own reflexes. Some of them coincide with these and some are different. I have found that these reflexes from TBM and CRA have proven to be accurate and served me well.

Organ reflexes are a reflection relating to the function of the system, organ, or gland to which they relate. When tested, using whatever system you choose, they give you a glimpse of the possible function or dysfunction of that system, organ, or gland.

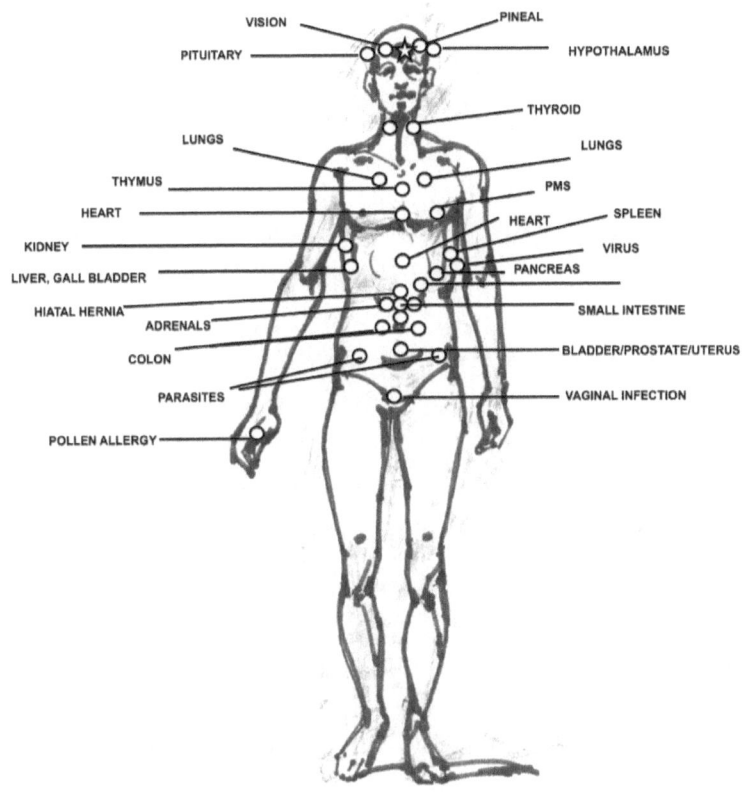

YOUR REFLEX POINTS

Your Energy Patterns

An example of the optimal energy pattern is when I energy test the entire body, and don't find any organ or gland reflexes at all. In addition, I can have the person localize their organ or gland and we still do not find any reflexes, and their symptoms are basically gone. They are in a balanced and most favorable state of overall health.

A weakened energy pattern could manifest through any number of physical, mental or emotional discomforts such as intestinal pain, bloating, gas, heartburn, skin rash, anxiety, insomnia, waking up at certain times of the night, which would mean that the person's circadian clock may be off.

A severely impacted energy pattern could be indicated through a myriad of more serious symptoms. I had a case where the patient had been to a few doctors, and no one was able to help her. She was in another dimension, was psychologically reversed, she even had brain disorganization where her right and left hemispheres were not communicating. She was switched from a general energy standpoint.

Through my testing process, I found about six or seven different organ and gland dysfunctions in her. She had Intestinal problems, multiple joint pain and anxiety. Her energy pattern was in serious distress.

The Circadian Clock

All the organs and glands rejuvenate at certain times of the day or night. If they are in the process or rejuvenating, but are having trouble doing that because they are stressed in some way, they will cause anxiety in the body and that will result in the person basically waking up.

For example, the liver commences the regeneration process at 1AM that is on going until 3AM. If a person is waking up during this time, it indicates that the liver is dysfunctional and is causing the person to wake up.

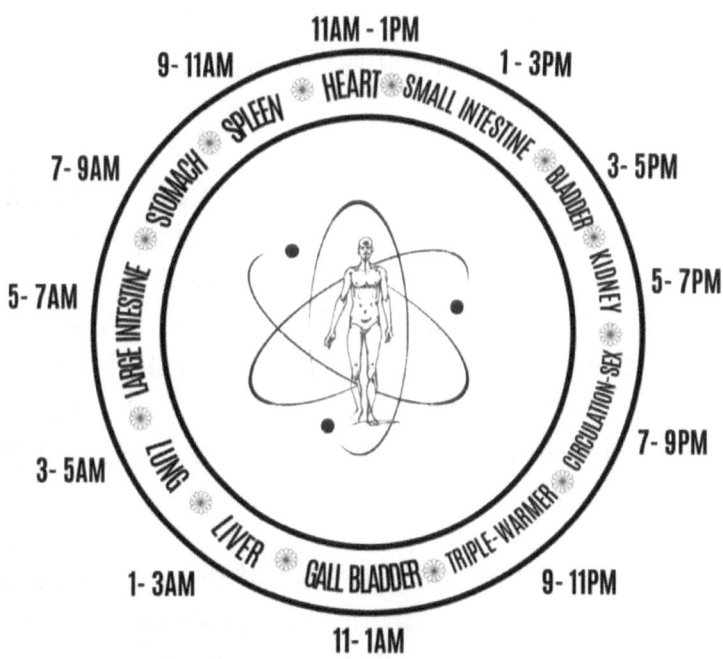

The Adrenals

Adrenals are probably one of the most important glands in the body, simply because they help regulate your metabolism, immune system, blood pressure, response to stress, as well as the sodium potassium balance in your system. They are composed of the cortex and the medulla, each responsible for producing different hormones.
The adrenals are absolutely the first line of defense against any stress that we experience.

This was proven by Vienna-born pioneering endocrinologist Hans Selye (1907-1982) in all of his work when he developed the GAS - general adaptor syndrome, describing the three predictable stages of body's response to stressors; alarm, resistance and exhaustion.

With my patients, I frequently see the adrenals as a challenge that seems to be overlooked by the medical profession. Unfortunately, there is no medical test for adrenal function, except evaluation for Addison's disease or extreme adrenal dysfunction which requires medication. We have the cortisol test, but unfortunately that doesn't reveal the actual state of the adrenals.

When I explain to my patients what seems to be their challenge, I define and formulate for them what Hans Selye said about the different stages. I then determine if the patient is in the alarm, the resistant, or the exhaustion stage.

Most of the people that I see are in the exhaustion stage which creates anxiety, depression and fatigue, with a general inability to manage the challenges of daily life.

I think that the amount of stress in our society today is creating a plethora of adrenal problems, and we can't seem to get out of the alarm stage. What Hans Selye defined, was the complex dynamic of alarm and consecutively the resistance stage, which is supposed to be the recuperative stage where you have an opportunity to rebound from the alarm stage. But he mentions, that if you cannot get out of the initial alarm stage, the resistance stage eventually ends up in the final exhaustion stage, and this is precisely when you begin having various physiological problems.

The most common challenge with adrenals is the adrenal fatigue. Stress of every kind can cause adrenal fatigue and adrenal burnout. Like Hans Selye said, there are countless stressors. They can be emotional, physical, or even severe temperature fluctuations can cause stress.

Since the adrenals help us deal with whatever stress we are experiencing, it is also important to understand that stress is in a lot of ways necessary and does to a degree strengthen our bodies. However, if stress becomes overwhelming and chronic, it definitely creates a problem. This is when the adrenal fatigue occurs.

Everyone has experienced fatigue, but not everybody will experience the accompanying anxiety or depression. Hans Selye found that the cause for depleted adrenals can be emotional or physical, such as in the case of a marathon runner. Too much exercise can weaken the adrenals, because they are simply under too much stress. Similarly, a person that is in a very hot environment is in danger of putting the adrenals under a great amount of stress, because they have to react and adapt to the heat or extreme cold.

In fact, the adrenals have to respond quickly to any kind of stress that the body is facing. In my practice, I find that food allergies, viruses and certainly emotions are a very big factor in adrenal stress. There can be any number of triggers that are constantly weakening the adrenals, so when one experiences an unexpected major emotional stressor such as a surgery, divorce, job loss, or any occurrence that pushes them over the edge, they end up suffering from major symptoms.

It could be stress on the adrenals, the liver, the pancreas, the thyroid, or any number of areas that are being overly stressed so that the body has to use extra energy to compensate. As a result, it simply fails to maintain the balance that it needs, in order to adapt to life.

To a large degree the focus of my work is to find out what is triggering the body to use so much energy that it can't maintain itself. Identifying the problem gives my patients hope. Most often they have been to several medical doctors who couldn't figure out what is going on. Perhaps the medical tests seemed fine, and several practitioners tried various approaches, but nothing seemed to work. These people lose hope that anyone will ever find the cause of what is going on with them. They begin to capitulate and accept that this is the way they will feel and function for the rest of their life.

When they come to see me and I conduct a thorough observation and assessment, I explain to them their overwhelming symptoms: anxiety, high blood pressure, severe fatigue, hair loss, hyper sensitivity to light, and digestive problems. It certainly becomes quite obvious that the liver, thyroid, adrenals, small and large intestine are out of balance.

People quickly realize there is no wonder they have all these symptoms. It triggers their brain to recognize the clear reason why they are feeling so terrible. Through my process, I narrow it down and promptly determine that the adrenals are the priority, and we immediately begin to work on that.

Because the adrenals can cause weakness in the ligaments and general joint pain and back problems, the patient may go to a chiropractor and end up eventually discovering their difficulties are all caused by adrenals. In this book, I am focusing on the adrenal challenge, and this information can be of great benefit also to chiropractors, precisely because of that fact.

When you do have these kinds of symptoms and suspect that the adrenals may be your problem, I suggest you visit the TBM (Total Body Modification) website at www.livetbm.com and find a qualified doctor in your area. Some of the additional long-term consequences of adrenal burnout are a lowered immune system, various allergies, chronic fatigue, poor concentration, and brain fog.

It is important to mention, that the adrenal fatigue will also cause thyroid fatigue, because the thyroid may try to over compensate for the general state of low energy that the adrenals are producing. So eventually, you will begin to suffer from thyroid burnout as well. You could also experience diabetes, since the adrenals are responsible for controlling the balance of blood sugar. It is important to note that adrenal vulnerability can also be hereditary.

MILD ADRENAL BURNOUT

The first signs that your adrenals may be in trouble are fatigue and not having any energy to do the things you want to do. A mild adrenal burnout can be indicated with weight gain, particularly around the midriff area, fatigue, sleeplessness, or waking up often during the night.

At this point people usually get some sleep medicine to try to compensate for the discomfort. There may be some bouts of depression that could also be caused by the adrenals, or the liver. The adrenals and the liver are very interactive, and I often find them to affect each other. Diarrhea is also a sign of adrenal dysfunction, because of the body's water imbalance. In a case where the adrenals were affecting my patient's liver, the muscle testing indicated the liver was dysfunctional. Once I corrected the adrenals, the liver bounced back and regained its strength.

SEVERE ADRENAL BURNOUT

A serious state of adrenal burnout is when a person is experiencing a profound fatigue and anxiety. An even greater severe adrenal burnout is indicated when a person is afraid of everything and simply can't recover, while feeling perpetually on edge. This state also involves and affects many organs, not be just one or two, but more likely five or six. In a case of severe adrenal burnout, numerous organs are involved

The extreme burnout is called Addison's syndrome. In such a case the adrenals are completely burned out and one has to resort to medication. Unfortunately, this condition does not offer the possibility for full recovery. If it is not treated and corrected, a person could die within two or three days. Addison's disease requires ongoing medication for a lifetime, in order to substitute for the lack of hormones.

COPING MECHANISM

The onset of adrenal burnout usually begins with fatigue, then some anxiety, sleeplessness, and diarrhea. In the case of severe adrenal fatigue, usually the blood pressure drops. This is called orthostatic hypotension. When you stand up or sit up quickly from a lying or sitting position, your blood pressure is supposed to go up, in order to compensate for the lack of oxygen getting to the brain. If the adrenals are severely burned out, that doesn't occur, and as a result, the patient experiences dizziness and incidents of vertigo.

ADRENAL BURNOUT AND CHRONIC FATIGUE

The chronic fatigue is often associated with adrenal fatigue. Because of the stress and the chemicals the adrenals produce, they cause a lot of overall weakness in the muscles, and general body pain.

Additionally, when the adrenals get out of balance, the muscles and ligaments get very weak. There is a lot of joint discomfort and much overall instability in the joints.

When someone has extreme adrenal fatigue, they often experience a lot of physical pain in several different joints and areas in their body. When I help the adrenals to work properly, the pain considerably subsides. My focus is to do whatever is necessary to get the triggers off.

ADRENAL FATIGUE IN VARIOUS AGE GROUPS

Adrenal fatigue in children manifests as anxiety. Men and women with adrenal fatigue exhibit the same kinds of symptoms. It can certainly affect the hormone cycle. Most likely the pituitary gland will be affected as well. Adrenal burnout in elderly depends on the amount of stress that they are experiencing, and it takes longer for their body to respond and rebuild the gland, as opposed to a younger person.

ADRENAL FATIGUE AND ANXIETY

Many patients come to me with severe stress. They are usually given drugs and are undergoing counseling, and in every single case I find that they are suffering from adrenal dysfunction. Once I assist them in getting the adrenals to function properly, the anxiety goes away in two weeks.

The state of anxiety is certainly related to the adrenals. People experience stress for a variety of different reasons and they certainly need to look at that and make an effort to minimize the stress. A state of fight or flight puts one in a sympathetic dominance.

SYMPATHETIC AND PARASYMPATHETIC NERVOUS SYSTEM

There are two aspects to the autonomic nervous system. The nervous system relating to the parasympathetic and sympathetic is the autonomic nervous system or ANS, which is responsible for regulating the body's unconscious actions. Sympathetic system is part of the fight or flight mechanism. Parasympathetic system is responsible for activities that occur when the body is at rest. When under stress, you are continuously getting into the sympathetic part of the nervous system. This causes the destruction of the organs and glands since they are under constant barrage of the stress hormones. I focus on helping patients return into their parasympathetic system, so they can relax, heal and get their lives back.

OCCASIONAL STRESS VERSUS CHRONIC STRESS

With only occasional stress, you will not experience the negative symptoms, because the adrenals will switch on, the heart rate will go up, and you will basically experience the fight or flight mechanism, which is the adrenals activating to handle the acute stress. This mechanism in our body helps us to fight for our life or run away from danger.

As Hans Selye describes, the resistant stage is where the parasympathetic portion of our nervous system kicks in, and basically heals the body from that alarm stage, while replenishing chemicals. Unless you are exceptionally sensitive to your body, you most likely won't notice a big difference other than the stress has passed and you feel calm and relaxed. You sense that your body is properly healing and recovering.

ADRENAL RECOVERY

Recovery from adrenal burnout depends on the actual level of burnout. However, the recovery from *chronic* adrenal burnout is possible, but it will take probably three to five months to really completely recover. The adrenals require a long restorative time. Any organ that the body needs to rebuild, takes adequate time to sufficiently strengthen and return to functioning on its own. I use nutritional supplements to help support the gland until the body can return to properly functioning on its own.

If you are under a lot of stress, it is going to continuously deplete the adrenals and present an ongoing challenge.

When you ignore your stress levels and remain under chronic stress, you will be losing too much sodium from your system.

The adrenals produce aldosterone, which then goes to the kidneys. The aldosterone causes the kidneys to reabsorb sodium and leach out potassium, and that maintains the proper balance in the fluid system of the body.

When you stand up quickly, the blood pressure can use that extra fluid to go up, so more oxygen gets to the brain. But if the adrenals are really fatigued and the aldosterone is not being produced properly, then actually the sodium levels go way down and the potassium levels go way up, and you become more dehydrated. In such case, the blood pressure then drops considerably. This is the reason why when you get to such extreme circumstances and the aldosterone is really eliminated, you are in danger of dying within two to three days. With all that extra potassium in your system, your heart goes into shock and spasm.

REMEDIES

I often meet patients who are taking herbal remedies for adrenals, and that is helpful, but I am afraid it serves more like a band aid. If you don't remove the triggers that are impairing the adrenals, then the band aid is only going to be helpful periodically and temporarily. When I am working with a patient, I try to find what is actually causing the adrenals to weaken. These triggers could be an emotional situation, old hidden anger from their childhood, food allergies, heavy metals, fungus, chemicals they may be exposed to on a regular basis, or even Epstein-Barr virus. It could be any number of things.

If I don't eliminate those triggers, it will be challenging to get the adrenals to function normally. I usually eliminate them through the technique called harmonization process, so that the body no longer reacts to them. Next, I use nutritional supplements or a chelation agent depending on whatever the trigger is, to help eliminate it from the body.

Rebuilding the organ requires nutrition from a glandular extract unless the person is vegan, in such a case I use the homeopathic version. I try to go to a bovine adrenal. The body is not species specific, it is tissue specific. It only cares that it is adrenal or whatever tissues is used. There are several herbs that will to some degree stimulate the adrenals, such as ginseng and Ashwagandha.

I usually don't rely on herbs as much, because they are more of a stimulant, as opposed to rebuilding.

The tissue organ nutrition actually causes the body to rebuild the organ or gland while strengthening it.
I have seen better long-term results with those.

CASE STUDY I.

I had a case with a woman patient, who suffered from anxiety and various problems. She had about six organ systems that were dysfunctional, but the priority was her adrenals. When I asked her body what was going on with her adrenals, it responded that there was a lot of anger, fear, despair, and hopelessness concerning her body, because she was so dysfunctional she could hardly do anything.

So I asked her:
"Was there some anger or fear in childhood?"
She replied: "Oh my God, the whole childhood was filled with anger and fear."
So that was a major component we had to work on, to help her adrenals to finally kick in and work at 100% like its supposed to.

CASE STUDY II.

A client came to me a few months ago from a referral. She had been to the Cleveland clinic and to various doctors. She suffered from massive pain all over her body, extreme anxiety, depression, and was feeling quite miserable.

Working with her, I found her in the 7th dimension. Her underlying emotions were fear and anger. I found the adrenals affecting about eight other organs. She had Candida, Epstein Barr virus in three different forms, three food allergies, a pituitary dysfunction, and all her hormones were off.

I was able to correct the candida, Epstein Barr virus and one of her food allergies, diffuse her emotional disturbance, and correct the pituitary.
At the conclusion, I gave her nutritional supplements for support.
When I called her the next day and she exclaimed:
" I haven't felt this good in years!"
This turnaround happened in just one day.

CASE STUDY III.

I had a six-years old patient brought in to see me by her grandmother. The little girl was on three different anti-anxiety drugs, which was really quite upsetting.
I found some emotional issues such as anger, a few food allergies and candida.

We addressed food allergies and candida during the first couple of visits. Her anxiety had dropped so much that within a few weeks she was able to get off all her drugs. She still had some emotional issues left over, and I asked her what was causing her anger. Her answer was simple:" My brother!"

We did some acupower, which takes a certain amount of concentration, and her anxiety totally went away. Since then, she has been anxiety- free.

The Thyroid

The Thyroid gland is the number one controller of metabolics in the body. It produces hormones that control the speed of your metabolism and therefore acts as the body's metabolic regulator.
Since thyroid controls the body temperature, a very revealing question to determine the state of thyroid would be:" Are you feeling cold all the time?"

One of the most common symptoms with a challenged thyroid are loss of hair, outer third of the eyebrow is lacking hair growth, edema or swelling around or particularly underneath the eyes, dry skin, constipation, speeding of heart rate, foggy brain, weight gain, and fatigue, usually in mid-afternoon time. With the adrenal burnout you feel tired in the morning, and with the thyroid problems I find that the patients are experiencing a low energy state in the afternoon.

Often women will experience hormonal problems or infertility. A serious thyroid imbalance can manifest as obesity, depression, high cholesterol levels, low energy, and chronic fatigue.

The medical profession standard of rule anytime they suspect a thyroid dysfunction is a TSH blood test that measures this hormone to find out if your thyroid gland is working the way it should. I found that the TSH basically indicates that the thyroid is functioning, but it doesn't tell you how well it's functioning.

You can have someone with normal TSH that could still be hypothyroid. Therefore you really need to examine a lot of physical signs as well and combine the blood work. If someone comes to me with a TSH test that seems normal, I ask them to go back to their medical doctor and have them do a full panel on the thyroid, the T4, T 3, and even an RT3 so I can see how the thyroid is actually functioning, as opposed to the fact that it's just working.

Even though I find that the pituitary has been the primary gland that I use when I find that someone has been having problems with infertility, the thyroid can have a lot to do with it as well. I stimulate the thyroid, which has a direct link to the sexual glands and the sexual hormones, which has a profound effect on overall hormonal balance in the body.

If the problem is a hyperthyroid condition, then one would experience a whole other set of symptoms, such as racing heartbeat, hyper metabolism, constant nervousness and anxiety. I would again look at the adrenals, because the adrenals and thyroid have a very strong and intimate relationship. If the adrenals are down then the thyroid is going to try to kick in and support the body, particularly the energy, and it may go into a hyper state like hyperthyroid, just because it's trying to compensate for a low adrenal problem.

A hypothyroid person will also have a low body temperature. That is one of the tests that you can do, other than a blood test. It's actually in a lot of ways more accurate to take the metabolic temperature other than the blood test. Nervousness could be caused by the hyperthyroid, but if a person has low energy, even though they are feeling nervous all the time, and have anxiety, it could be caused by the adrenals, which need to be checked. They could be drawing energy from the thyroid and causing the hypothyroid. I see that quite often.

I don't find the thyroid as being the main gland in the body's problems, I oftentimes find the adrenals being the primary, and they are affecting the thyroid, if the thyroid does come up in my scan. I very seldom find the vice versa where the thyroid is the primary, and causing the adrenal fatigue.

The main challenges that can cause a thyroid problem are the adrenals and autoimmune disease. A blood test is advised to detect if there is an increase in the antigen activity. Antigens are toxins or other foreign substances, which induce an immune response in the body. This often occurs from a leaky gut problem that is the main cause of all autoimmune diseases. Thyroid imbalance is often camouflaged as something else, or misdiagnosed as chronic fatigue. Thyroid vulnerability can also be hereditary.

Recovery from thyroid imbalance depends on how severe it has gotten. In early stage you can support thyroid recovery with various nutritional supplements. In severe cases, one may need to take medication for the rest of their life.

My approach to healing thyroid imbalance is to go back to what I do as far as looking at all the different organs and glands and find out what the priority is. Oftentimes the adrenals are the root cause, so that is were the healing process begins.

I oftentimes have to give thyroid supplementation. I very seldom find a food allergy with the thyroid, or a trigger from that standpoint. It is more often the case of pituitary not producing enough TSH because the pituitary is off, or there's a dysfunction from the antigen area autoimmune. I do have a real problem with pharmaceutical synthetic T4 and they will stimulate the thyroid to a certain degree but they convert to T3 very poorly in the body.

And any time you supplement a hormone or a secretion that an organ or a gland is supposed to be producing, as a result, the body will weaken that gland. It simply doesn't use it anymore, because you're getting that same supplementation through a pharmaceutical state. I find people that have been on synthroid for long periods of time have very weak thyroids. I usually suggest to them to talk to their medical doctors and switch to glandular which actually works a lot better for them because it contains a T4 and T3.

The problem is that the majority of the thyroid supplementation are not allowed to have T3 in them. This is the difference between a prescription and a supplement.

All you can do is the glandular, which may be able to stimulate the thyroid sufficiently to produce its own T3 better, and I often use glandulars precisely for that purpose. However, if someone has a really weak thyroid, then I simply recommend they go to a medical doctor and see if they can get on a natural or glandular prescription with T3 and T4.

If someone's challenge with the thyroid is caused by the adrenals, once you restore the adrenals the thyroid could reactivate and recover. Similarly, if the pituitary is the cause, when it gets balanced, the thyroid can reactivate and recover. It all depends on the source and degree of the problem.

If the thyroid is weakened because the patient has been for years on synthroid, it may not be able to recover. You may be able to get it stronger, but you still may have to have some support.

The other thing that I find as a key factor, is RT 3 which stands for reversed T3. The reversed T3 is the incomplete conversion of T4 to T3. It's kind of like a waste product, it has the exact same configuration as T3, but it has no physiological function in the body.

So it still can adhere to the receptors at the cell level, but it has no physiological function so it acts like garbage plugging up the cell receptor.

There is going to be a certain amount of RT3 established, it's not going to be across the board perfect.

Because the body is not getting the T3 that it needs, it's constantly signaling the thyroid to produce more T4, and it can weaken the thyroid. Total Body Modification (TBM) does have a treatment for RT3.

Often one can recover and have their thyroid return to normal functioning within five to six months.
The key remedies and actions that help you recover from thyroid imbalance are a healthy diet and several nutrition supplements that help stimulate the body to rebuild the gland naturally.

The Pituitary

The pituitary gland has an intimate connection with the thyroid gland and controls the function of most other endocrine glands, and is therefore often called the master gland.

If the pituitary gland is not functioning properly, the person is experiencing a general sense of weakness and once it is adjusted, they feel overall sense of wellbeing. The clearest indicator that a woman's pituitary gland is challenged, are various imbalances with sexual hormones that the pituitary gland controls. Without its proper function the ovaries and the entire reproductive system is challenged. If a patient is experiencing infertility, a weak pituitary may be failing to stimulate the ovaries to release the egg. Once the pituitary is stabilized, I've seen very effective positive results with conquering infertility.

To find the cause of health challenges, I muscle test all glands. Most of the time the pituitary is acting independently and I have to address it separately.

There is a cranial adjustment that I suggest in order to adjust the pituitary that is very effective. It is easy and I teach my patients to adjust it on their own. Often the adjustment of pituitary offers considerable help in cases of various problems with the menstrual cycle. Addressing the pituitary will help regulate it back to a normal state.

When I see my patients I help adjust the pituitary for them, but that may not be sufficient and they will need to adjust it on their own as well. This way they can help keep in functioning properly for a length of time that is sufficient for the body to make the needed changes in order for the menstrual cycle to get back to functioning properly.

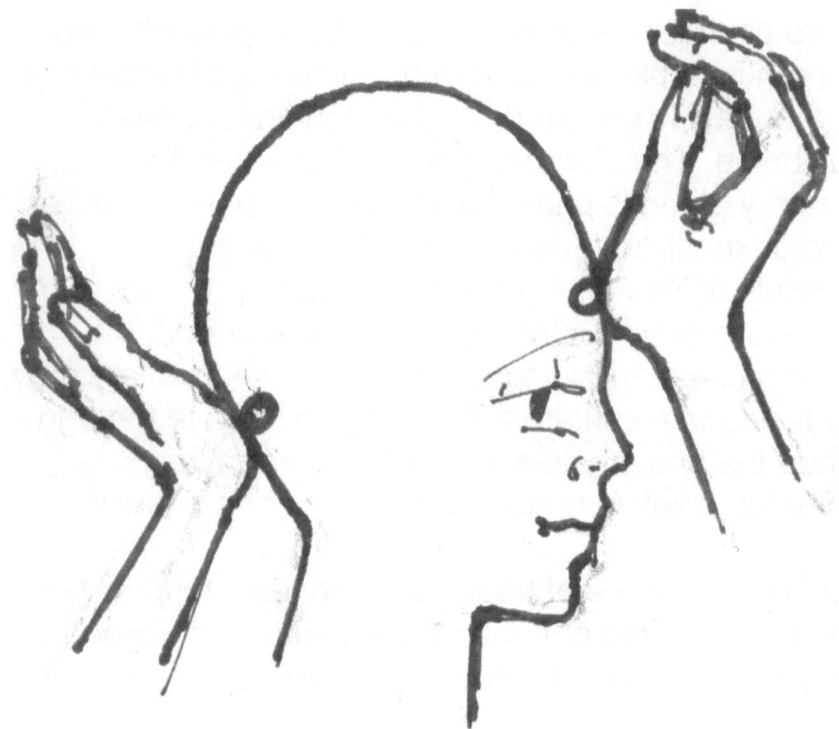

PITUITARY ADJUSTMENT

Place your hand at the base of your skull at the back, just above the top of the neck, and place your other hand over the third eye and squeeze the two hands together, while taking a deep inhale and holding it for three counts. Next, exhale and release the hands. Repeat this process seven times.

Food Allergies

Food allergies in today's society are to a certain degree a direct result of unhealthy food filled with chemicals. But a person could be eating the best organic foods and still have a food allergy. As an example, many people are allergic to dairy, and even if it is the most pure organic dairy they can find, they are simply allergic to all dairy, whether organic or homogenized. It doesn't seem to matter, the body reacts to dairy itself.

Allergies are definitely worse now than they were in the past. In addition, having higher stress levels that people are under on a regular basis, perpetuates more allergies. People's lives are generally more stressful in regards to their work situation, political environment that we see in the country and the world in general, as well as ongoing time spent on cellphones, internet and social media. All these elements present very high stressors for people.

In general, the speed at which people are living today is hyped and society demands a very high level of involvement, and considerably less time dedicated to relaxation and downtime.

I don't find all allergies affecting the intestinal track. Often they present challenges for various organs like the liver, adrenals, thyroid and pancreas. In such cases people are often unaware that they suffer from a food allergy.

Nowadays I find a lot more gluten allergies than I used to, in fact almost everyone has some level of gluten sensitivity.
Another factor is of course the diet, if a person constantly consumes the same kind or type of food, they can develop an allergy to that food. This is of course more common if they have also been under a lot of stress.

The adrenals have a lot to do with allergies because they are dealing with stress on the body and that can affect the metabolism. The most allergy triggering foods are corn, gluten, dairy, eggs and nightshades.

If the person suffers from a physical ailment, there will almost always be an association with a food allergy as well. High levels of candida are also strongly associated with food allergies. General toxicity in the body likewise seems to make people more sensitive to foods.

Another factor is stress, because it affects the liver, which has the responsibility to filter the allergens out of the blood. If the liver is dysfunctional it simply can not manage and fulfill that task.

Allergic reactions to foods have to do with each individual's general state of health. Allergies rob the body of energy that it needs to maintain the proper healthy balance. Food allergy can be the trigger to cause a weak liver, adrenals or any other organ.

This weakness creates other issues like intestinal

problems, depression or in case of food allergies triggering adrenals, the patient can suffer from anxiety.

The best way to determine if you have food allergies is a blood test, which is by far the most accurate. My correlation of blood test and muscle test matches quite correctly. I believe that the skin sensitivity test for allergies is often simply inaccurate. In case of pollen allergies the skin test may list practically all plant life as a trigger. When I test the same patient, we will be able to narrow it down to plant or tree specifics that are considerably lower and more exact.

In case of a skin test, I believe the body goes into a state of hyper reaction and anything that you put on the body thereafter is going to cause your body to react in a hyper way. In contrast with the blood test, we can measure slight, moderate or extreme activity and narrow down your allergic reaction to the degree of accuracy. This is why I highly recommend the actual blood test to determine your allergies.

To heal and overcome the allergy challenge, the standard approach by medical doctors and naturopaths is the process of food elimination. This is certainly difficult, especially if the list of foods that one is allergic too is rather large.

I use a harmonization technique to help the body eliminate the food allergy which then allows the adrenals to recover and function more effectively. Once the body is harmonized to the food that was causing an allergic reaction, they no longer have that allergy and can actually consume that food a few hours after the harmonization process without experiencing any negative reactions whatsoever.

The harmonization process reprograms the body to no longer see the problematic food as a foreign substance and thus stops reacting to it in a negative way. I can only address three items at a time, so this healing process may require a few visits.

In case of challenging food and pollen allergies, I would recommend to the reader to find a qualified TBM practitioner.

Anaphylactic shock is an extreme allergy reaction and a life threatening medical emergency. Therefore whenever I harmonize a patient to a food that they know they have an anaphylactic reaction to, I always tell them to never eat that food after the treatment without their EpiPen.

Parasites

A parasite is an organism that lives and feeds on its host. Most people that have parasites can actually feel them in their body or see them in their stool. We can get parasites from under-cooked meat or raw fish, while traveling to foreign countries, or interacting with animals.

First I test the parasite reflex to find out if a parasite is present. If the muscle testing confirms the presence of parasites, I have numerous vials that can be used in the harmonization process and to determine what kind.

One typical sign indicating the presence of parasites is diarrhea. Another important fact is to find out where the parasites are lodging, as they are often times in the lungs or the liver.

Most of the time they are in the colon and one will easily notice diarrhea, pain, gas and bloating.

Very effective herbs for elimination of parasites are garlic and oregano oil as well as various homeopathic remedies.

When my patients plan to travel to a foreign land, I often supply them with emulsified oregano as a preventative measure.

Mold

Mold is a very powerful fungi that grow in filaments and reproduces by forming spores that can travel through the air. Mold can literally destroy the body. I have seen people that were living in a house full of mold, and their health was simply ruined.

To help with a mold issue, I use the harmonizing technique on a patient's body, but if they return to the house full of mold, that mold will overtake them yet again. It is too powerful and cannot be controlled. It is best to move out of a residence that has mold issues. Fortunately, not all structures have mold.

If a person discovers that they have an issue with mold, I suggest they find a TBM practitioner as well as an acupuncturist as the combination of those two modalities often offers much relief and brings about positive results.

Fungus

I find fungus in my patients in various areas of the body, showing up as hives, skin lesions, or chronic cough. The most common type of fungus that can spread by wind is found in environment, including soil, plant matter and is called Aspergillus fumigatus. There are many kinds of fungus, such as dangerous Aflatoxin that causes liver cancer and is fairly common.

If your immune system is strong, your body is resistant to fungus, but nevertheless it can manifest as a slow growing issue and the immune system won't recognize the challenge. I had a patient that was diagnosed with lesions on her lungs that were caused by a fungus. Slow growing fungus can hide in the body for a very long time without being detected. A common toe fungus can likewise be very destructive and can spread from toes to other interior parts of the human body. If the fungus is not causing the typical symptoms, it can be lodged in an organ and causes dysfunction of that organ without actually manifesting the typical symptoms.

I use the harmonizing technique as an immediate remedy for fungus, because it stops the body from reacting. If the fungus remains in the body even though the body is not violently reacting to it, the fungus still needs to be eliminated. In such a case, I use anti-fungal remedies for a certain period of time after the initial harmonizing therapy.

Candida

Candida is a yeast that grows in the intestinal track and is part of our digestive system. The microbiom is the bacteria that inhabits the large and small intestines which competes with candida and maintains a healthy gut flora. This can only occur if the microbiom is healthy. However, if a patient has undergone a regimen of antibiotics which kill-off the microbiom, and new probiotics are not introduced into the system, the candida multiplies extremely fast and takes control.

The symptoms of having candida, as far as the digestive system, can be bloating and pain. If candida resides in an organ or throughout the body, it can cause depression, various rashes, and constant craving for sweets, carbs and sweet fruit. It requires great self-discipline to control this kind of craving.

Candida also makes it almost impossible to lose weight. In extreme cases it is not effective to manage candida with probiotics.

Harmonization is initially very effective, followed by an intense regimen of probiotics. I suggest a double dose for at least a week, afterwards continue with a daily dose for three to four months. This will help build up the intestinal flora, so that it can maintain the control of candida and help rebuild a healthy microbiom. An herb that is also very effective for eliminating candida is oregano oil.

Lyme disease

I generally see Lyme disease cases years down the line, when they manifest as a chronic illness. I have less patients in acute, first onset stage.

The first visible characteristic sign after a person has been bitten by a tick, is a bulls eye rash. It usually happens within the first two to three days after the initial bite. The next indication signs are flu like symptoms with headache, nausea, fatigue and fever.

Later on, most people develop some sort of muscle and joint pain that seems to migrate throughout the body. The pain does not present itself like an injury, where a specific joint or area continuously hurts. It may be the shoulder one day, and the hip the next, knees or feet, the pain just sort of migrates around the body from joint to joint. The patient complains that they hurt all over.

A lot of these symptoms mimic other organ problems. That's actually one of the challenges that I have with treating Lyme patients, because once I get through the Lyme protocol and vials no longer come up, which in my opinion means the disease is gone, people continue to come in and say they are still experiencing fatigue and hurt all over. I associate that with cleaning the remaining consequences and Lyme residue. Lyme disease causes great damaging effects on the liver, adrenals, thyroid and the brain. Patients come in with these symptoms that may take another six months to clear up. The body has to be "rebuilt", especially if they suffered from Lyme over a longer period of time.

One of the classic signs that the medical doctors use is the presence of a severe headache. That is troublesome, because it can also indicate meningitis, which can actually be caused by Lyme. Severe headaches can be a more serious chronic symptom. I refer patients to get checked for meningitis.

In a very small percentage of population some people will get bells palsy and have paralysis on one side of their face. Lyme disease can cause irregular heartbeat, peripheral neuropathy, sharp stabbing pain and burning and can attack the whole nervous system. It brings on extremely severe inflammation, which can cause enlargement and inflammation of the liver, and results in hepatitis.

Another common consequence is arthritis, which has to do with general inflammation.
Most disturbing is the danger of actual cognitive dysfunction, such as short-term memory and problems with decision making. If someone suddenly displays these symptoms, you have to question them if they have been bitten by a tick.

Another symptom is sensitivity to light, which is similar to adrenal dysfunction. Lyme disease affects many different organs and glands, with symptoms that can cross over.

It can directly affect the heart causing Lymes carditis, when Lyme bacteria enters the heart tissue and causes inflammation. Some of the symptoms are enlargement of the heart and chest pain.

Lyme Treatment Protocol

I have had a few patients with lots of body pain, foggy brain, and one of the things that I will ask the body with muscle testing about what is ailing it:
"What's going on? Is this Lyme disease?"
If the body responds with a "Yes", then I place the Lyme vials on the body and test them. Usually they will react strongly, which confirms to me an accurate diagnosis.

I examine my patients with my specific Lyme vials kit that has the Lyme and all co-infections, and find it to be very accurate for indicating the disease may exist within the patient's body. The blood tests are unfortunately very unreliable and the disease is very difficult to detect. Quite often I see a case where the medical doctors assert there is no Lyme, while the patient has all the classic symptoms, and the Lyme vials kit right away shows that the patient indeed has Lyme disease.

The program that I use takes about three to five months to correct its effects on the body, in addition to at least another six months for full recovery.
I initially have the patient place the Lyme vial kit on their body. If the muscle test displays a weakness, I have them place their finger on each vial.

Every time I get a weak muscle response, it is the body responding and confirming that specific Lyme co-infection is active in the body. I always recheck and retest the responses to make sure nothing is missed.

Next, I use the Total Body Modification technique to harmonize the body with the selected vials. It helps break that energetic connection that Lyme has to the body so it no longer reacts to Lyme disease. This allows the body to go after the illness and effectively kill off the bacteria.

Sometimes the patients will get a flu like reaction afterwards which is a detox response called herxeimer. I reschedule my patients to return after two to three weeks, because I found this is the amount of time it usually takes for another bacteria to become active.

When the patient returns, we will re-check all the vials and their body will usually select brand new ones. The vials we used the first time usually don't respond or indicate that the bacteria returned the second time. I repeat the process again after two to three weeks.

During the harmonization process we are raising the resonance of the body's identification to that particular bacteria, so that the resonance of the human body overpowers the frequency of the bacteria. When you raise the person's frequency, it overpowers the lower frequency, which ceases to exist.

Again, I want to remind you that recovery time depends on each individual's general condition.

CASE STUDIES

I had a patient who happens to be a homeopath. She was bitten by a tick and had a bulls-eye rash on her leg. It spread over the entire left side of her body and required three treatments to get improved.

In case of a five years old boy who was bitten on his arm, it required a few visits for recovery. I have seen him for the last three years and the Lyme disease never returned.

In a case where patient suffered from chronic Lyme, total depletion, lung problems and fungus, it took six months to get her improved. She is now problem free.

In several cases where patients were on antibiotics for two years, they still had active Lyme. I've only seen one person who actually got well after taking the antibiotics. Everybody else still had Lyme to a certain degree. After two years, just think of what damage that is doing to the rest of your body, the intestinal track and microbiome!

II.
Talk to Your Body

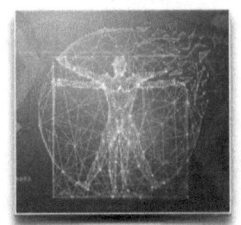

About Dimensions

In 2007 I had an experience with a patient that dramatically changed the way I approach my work, and I believe this has made a significant difference in my results. I am not sure what to call this unusual transformation or even its validity, all I know is that it has allowed me to tap deeper into my patient's emotional and metabolic work areas of dysfunction, that were previously not accessible.

In case of emotional issues, it has helped pry open the patient's deeper awareness of the problem with which they may be struggling. This technique has become one of the initial pre-screening questions that I ask the body through muscle testing, before pursuing anything else. It has become the guiding light that helps me find deep seated areas of dysfunction, especially in the more serious and complicated cases that come my way.

I am not sure how to explain this process or what it actually means, so I will begin with the description of events, that allowed me to discover this extraordinary method and establish my multi-dimensional protocol.

At that time, I had just finished reading *The Divine Matrix* by Gregg Braden. Shortly thereafter, I was working on an older patient who suffered from various digestive disorders. I had worked on her a few times before and felt we were making progress. However, on that day, she came into my office, complaining that the issue was bothering her again. I did my usual workup using a combination of Total Body Modification reflexes with Dr. Versendaal's CRA reflexes. Usually they will reveal an area of weakness or dysfunction that will clarify the direction that requires treatment. However, this time, all the reflexes were strong, giving no indication that anything was wrong. Yet, I had a patient who was clearly in distress. This did not make any sense.

So partly joking and practically irritated that I was unable to find the source of her challenge, I asked her body:
" What are you? In another dimension?"
When I retested the indicator muscle, it replied: "Yes."
Now, I was really confused. So I asked again, this time a bit more specifically:
"What dimension are you in?"
As I began counting, her body stopped me at the fourth dimension.
Without much reflection, I asked:
"Do I need to go there? Can you take me there?"
Her body again replied: "Yes."
Not knowing how I was going to even know how or when I got there, I just began counting, without a muscle test.
To my surprise, each time I went through a dimension, I sensed a powerful flush of energy that moved through my entire body. I had never experienced anything like this before, so it made me a bit uneasy.
When I got to the fourth dimension, which is where

her body said she was, the flush of energy I felt became more sustained. Since this felt different, I asked her body:
"Are we now in the fourth dimension?"
I got a strong muscle answer from her body: "Yes."

I was not sure what to do once I was in the fourth dimension, so I just proceeded to go through all of the reflexes again. This time, the responses were different. The liver, adrenals, small and large intestine reflexes were all positive. I continued with my usual routine and found that her liver was the priority.

As it turned out, all I needed to do was reset the liver, using the TBM techniques, as well as the iliosecal valve, which I always find dysfunctional if the liver is not operating properly.
Upon completion, I asked her body:
"Do we need to return to the present dimension?"
With a strong muscle test response it answered: "Yes."

I asked the body to take me back to the present and I experienced the same sensations, each time we descended through another dimension. I felt the powerful flush of energy, just as before, until we arrived at the present dimension, where again the energy burst felt more sustained. I did not share with the patient about what had just happened, but proceeded to ask her how long it usually took before she felt a discomfort after she ate a meal.
She replied: "About ten minutes."
So I gave her an energy bar, asked her to eat it while

resting in my waiting room, and wait for me until I finished working with my next patient. She did as I asked, and when I returned to the waiting room, she let me know that she was feeling just fine.

Next, I asked her to eat a normal meal that evening, and kindly call me the next morning, to let me know how she was doing.

The next morning, the phone rang and I heard her usually reserved voice, announce with a very cheerful demeanor:
"This was the first proper meal that I've eaten in weeks, and it did not upset my stomach!"
At this point I could not explain my unusual discovery, except that it had helped disclose an important dysfunction in my patient, that I could not find before in my normal course of evaluation.

In her case, this discovery played the key role in helping her with chronic digestive and stomach issues. Since that visit, I have found her in different dimensions on two other occasions. Each time, it was closely associated with very high levels of stress in her life.

Since that time and over the last twelve years, I have found numerous patients in other dimensions. Most often, a high degree of stress has preceded their visit with me, but in each case my initial observation did not pick up nearly as much information about their physical condition, as after I went to the dimension in which they were residing at that time.

I do not feel different when I go to the various other dimensions and neither do the patients. The only difference is, that while I am in the same dimension with the patient, I am able to pick up different areas of dysfunction that were not apparent before.

Working with Dimensions

We begin the process with the present dimension, and then follow with the first dimension, which is a different frequency. I cannot give you a clear answer about how many dimensions exist. I have found people in the 12th dimension, but that is quite rare. Usually they are in the 5th or 6th dimension.

There are different energy qualities that relate to each dimension. However, I don't want to know too many specifics about other dimensions, because I don't want it to jade my consciousness. My only interest is to find out what's wrong with a person in that dimension, and then help bring them back to the present, so that they don't have to "escape".

When I first started with my inter-dimensional work, I didn't even know what was going to happen.
I had no idea how I was ever going to know that I was in another dimension. But I received a very powerful sensory response.
When I said: "Number one." I sensed a very unusual and powerful rush of energy that went through my entire body.

I continued: "Number two..." and received another rush of energy, and every time I said the next dimension, I got this tremendous surge of power. When I got to number six, I sensed yet another tremendous rush of force, but it remained sustained, which was different.
At that point, I asked again:
"Am I in the sixth dimension?"
And the answer was affirmative, a strong: "Yes."

Through this technique, I believe I am working with the body's consciousness. If it is in another dimension or on a different frequency than I am, the body can't tell me what's really wrong with it. If I just stay in the present frequency space, and someone is in the sixth dimension, then I can't talk to their body, and they are simply unreachable. We are in two different frequency fields and delicate subtle energy communication is clearly not possible.

I believe in some cases people escape because of sheer need for survival. They get immensely stressed out in the present, so their body and their consciousness need to find a "safe haven", so to speak.

The downside of someone being in a different far away dimension is, that they feel awful all the time, and probably have a lot of symptoms. The biggest disadvantage is when they wish to get help from other practitioners, and they may not be able to receive very effective results. It certainly doesn't mean that the other practitioner's techniques are not good. The patient is simply in another dimension, and therefore inaccessible. The practitioner doesn't know that, and tries to treat them in the present, as expected.

The body is healthiest when focused in the present dimension. That's where it can function most effectively and be very adaptable to life. The way to transport to a different dimension with your patient, would be to first inquire from the patient through muscle testing if they are in fact in another dimension.

The patients do not realize that they are in another state of consciousness unless they are really confused, unfocused and disoriented. If a patient has a high level of awareness, they likely don't have a tendency to escape into another dimension or state of consciousness, because they are more present and self discerning.

While applying this method, I may be experiencing different frequencies of consciousness, or an altered state of reality. However, when I ask the patient's body if it is in another frequency or another dimension, it confirms and responds with "another dimension" and not frequency. That is the way the body relates to it.

Whatever it is, it seems to be giving me a deeper insight into the complex and intricate functions of the human body, both metabolically and emotionally.

Lately, I have been using this in emotional work with the Acupower, Dr. Durlacher's work, and the Core Belief, Dr. Kevin Millet's work. In both cases, I am able to find deeper emotional and core belief blocks, that I can't seem to find in the present dimension. When I take people to the dimension where these blocks reside, the patient can suddenly relate to them with great ease, and is very clear about what they are, as well as their place and time of origin. I then continue with the Acupower and Core Beliefs techniques with them, while we remain in their dimension.

I most often find patients in another dimension who have been to several doctors, and were unable to get any positive results. This is when they come to me.

CASE STUDY I.

A client I was working with had various issues. In the process, I had her place the hand on top of her head, and it was strong. Then I had her turn the hand over, and it was weak which was good, as it indicated to me that she was clearly not psychologically reversed. However for some reason, I had the impulse to go into dimension work with her.

I asked her body:
"Are you in another dimension?"
The body said: "Yes."
And I started counting: "Number one? Two?"
I continued to muscle test her each time I inquired about the next dimension.

When I arrived to number six, her muscle locked in, and I asked again:
"Are you in the sixth dimension?"
And the body answered: "Yes".
Finally, I said to the body:
"Take me to the sixth dimension."
And then I become very quiet and go deep within into complete stillness.

I had her put her hand on top of her head again, palm facing down, and this time it came up weak, which meant she was psychologically reversed.

Clearly, if I am not in the dimension that the patient is functioning in, I don't get the accuracy of the information that I need, in order to be able to work with their body and to be able to correct the imbalances that are there.

CASE STUDY II.

A case in point is one my patients that I was working with on a set of issues both metabolic and emotional. We had gained much progress with her in both areas. Towards the end of her treatment on one of her visits, she mentioned that she was still not able go to sleep without the use of medication.

I asked her, what she believed was the problem. She responded that each time she went to bed, she experienced a lot of anxiety. I asked her if she knew what could be the cause of her anxiety.

She responded with a simple and firm: "No".
Next, I asked her body if this issue was in another dimension.
It said:" Yes, it was in the sixth dimension."
After we went to the sixth dimension I asked her again what the anxiety was about. She immediately responded, that when she was young her grandfather would come in and sexually molest her at bedtime.

Using the Acupower system, we cleared this deep-set fear of being molested by her grandfather. A few days later, she reported to me that for the first time in years, she was now able to go to sleep without any help of the sleep medication. I have used the multi-dimensional method in many similar situations, especially when the patient had trouble relating to what and why they were feeling a certain way.

Muscle Testing

Muscle testing, which is also known as Applied Kinesiology, was developed in the 1960's by Dr. George Goodheart, a chiropractor from Michigan. He discovered that there was a relationship of certain muscle weaknesses associated with various organ and meridian points used by acupuncturists.
In my opinion, muscle testing or AK is not an end all diagnosis, but is a wonderful tool that can indicate organ and glandular problems and dysfunctions.

An accurate test requires clear intentions and honesty with the body. When you approach the muscle test, if you have intentions of specific wants the muscle test is going to reflect that belief system. That is where it can become inaccurate and that is probably why the medical profession doesn't accept it as a viable tool. Muscle testing can be influenced by a person's thoughts. You need to be absolutely clear minded and have no intentions whatsoever.

Muscle testing is a technique that requires practice. The more you establish the routine, the more accurate you will become. The most important point is that you cannot have any intention of the outcome. You are there to find out only what the body wants and needs. Predetermined intentions will interfere with the accuracy of those results. It comes down to the question and "Yes" or "No" answer, because the body cannot give you an opinion, it can only give you a straight answer. I always start the muscle testing session with testing the stress switches. When the person is really stressed out, their energy is somewhat scrambled and the body is not able to respond in a truly honest way as to what is happening. This is why the first test that I do is psychological reversal. When I test the body, and am asking my questions, I want the body totally focused on what it can do, so it can respond to me in a very focused way. As in "All right, I know what you are talking about and I can do this and you need to do that." But if it is stressed out, then the body is saying: "Well, I am dealing with something, I can't really tell you what to do, because I am so obsessed with what happened to me today."

How to Muscle Test

My purpose is not to teach you how to diagnose, but to teach and convey to you the fundamentals of muscle testing accurately, so you may use this method for nutritional needs, possible food sensitivities, and stress.

I stand on the side of the person. Many therapists stand in front of the person, but my opinion is that since everyone has an aura - energy field, it can interact between the patient and the therapist. If I stand right in front of the person, our governing meridians are interacting with each other. I don't want this to happen because their body could be responding to my energy more than necessary.

This is why I always stand at the side of the person and have them put their arm straight out in front of them.
We are using the anterior deltoid muscle, which is a small muscle, but we are not testing for strength.

Personally, I like to test with my dominant hand, because I feel I am more sensitive with that hand and I can feel the subtleties of the muscle locking or not locking.

Since you are standing on the right side of the person, you will use your right hand to test their left arm. Your palm and fingertips should be facing down. They are stretching their hand straight ahead in front of them.

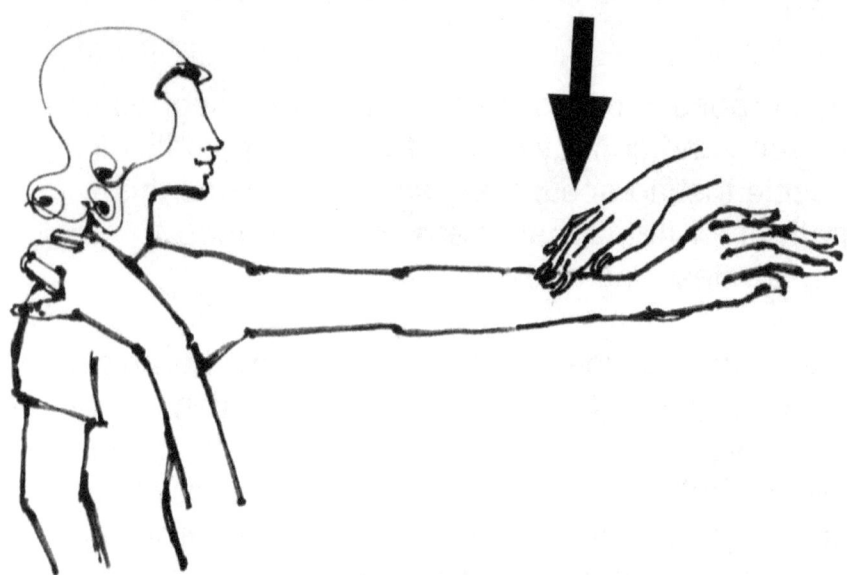

MUSCLE TEST

Place your hand on their wrist and then place your other hand on opposite shoulder to kind of stabilize them. Next, apply pressure, increasing slowly until you feel the muscle lock.

The big key at this point is you are not testing for strength, you are testing only for muscle function. You can have a young child, a weaker older person, or a strong young man, and if you were testing for strength, you would have trouble testing each one of those people. But if you are testing for function, everyone of those people will feel the same, and all you want them to do is to lock the muscle in.

You can test each of these different strength levels accurately, if you will let the person know that you want them to lock in their muscle. If the muscle does not lock, it will not feel solid but rather mushy and that means the muscle is dysfunctional, and not capable of locking.

If a person is too young or too old to test, for example a three year old, or someone very old and feeble or a person suffering from an illness that lacks in strength, then you can use another person to do the testing. This it is called *surrogate testing*. I explain this to people since I have a little bear in the office for that purpose.

When you contact both paws of the bear, it sings. If you let go of one of the paws, the bear stops singing because the current is broken. You could do this with one person or many people. One person is holding on to one paw, and another person to the other paw, and you could have fifty people holding hands connected to that second and first person. But if that fiftieth person is not hanging on to the person next to them, the bear will not sing. But as soon as the fiftieth person hangs on to the hand, the circuit is completed and the bear will sing. In surrogate testing all the other person has to do, is connect with the other person.

Therefore if you are testing a three-year old child, you could have the adult put their hand on the shoulder of that child and now you can test the other person, but get the information you need from the child. The weaker person you are testing can be even mentally absent, and you can still get the information you need using this technique.

I like to test with enough pressure so that I can consciously and physically tell when the muscle gives and cannot lock. This also allows the person being tested to feel the weakness. I believe this adds validity to the test for that person. If all of a sudden there is no locking and each test is weak, then I know the person has lost their focus on locking the muscle. I then have to ask the person to refocus on locking their muscle. This is the problem I find with very light muscle testing. If you are relying on your feelings of whether a muscle is locking or not, then I believe you have lost a certain amount of objectivity and validity with the other person.

Psychological Reversal

Psychological reversal is a state where the presence of a stressor has been so serious in a person's life, that it has scrambled their energy. Their brain can no longer function in a focused manner, and consequently their body is affected in a negative way as well.

I identify the state of psychological reversal with muscle testing. I have the patient place the palm of their hand on top of their head and test the muscle. The muscle response should be strong - locked. Next, they turn the hand over, and place the back of their hand on top of their head, and I retest the muscle. If the palm down on the top of their head is strong and the palm up is weak, that is the correct and healthy response.

But if the muscle testing response is just the opposite, the patient is in a state of psychological reversal, which is a subconscious condition of confusion. At that point the subconscious takes over and is making the decisions in that person's life and the conscious mind is no longer making decisions.

PSYCHOLOGICAL REVERSAL

STRONG

WEAK

HEALTHY STATE

WEAK

STRONG

The state of psychological reversal can be corrected with a simple exercise. Tap several fingers **on the outside of the actual fleshy side**, right before the little finger and repeat the following affirmation three times:

*"I deeply accept myself,
even though I feel terrible."*

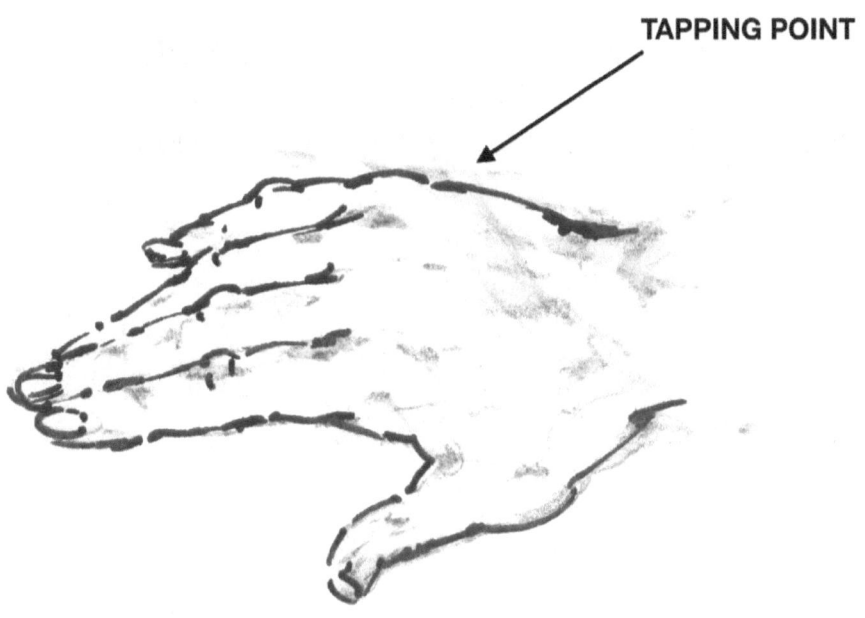

TAPPING POINT

When you say that phrase while tapping that acupuncture point, it reverses the negative state, and puts the conscious mind back in control.

This is a good exercise to do if you are feeling very stressed out by a situation, to help your body calm down and your mind become more focused.

Polarity Point

Place your finger right on the bridge of the nose, where the nose meets the forehead, and test the muscle. If it responds in a weak way, which it is supposed to do, then the body is testable and you can proceed with testing.
If it doesn't respond in a weak way and remains strong, then the polarity of the body is off.

How to fix the polarity of the body
You can reset the polarity by rubbing at C1 underneath the base of the skull on both sides.

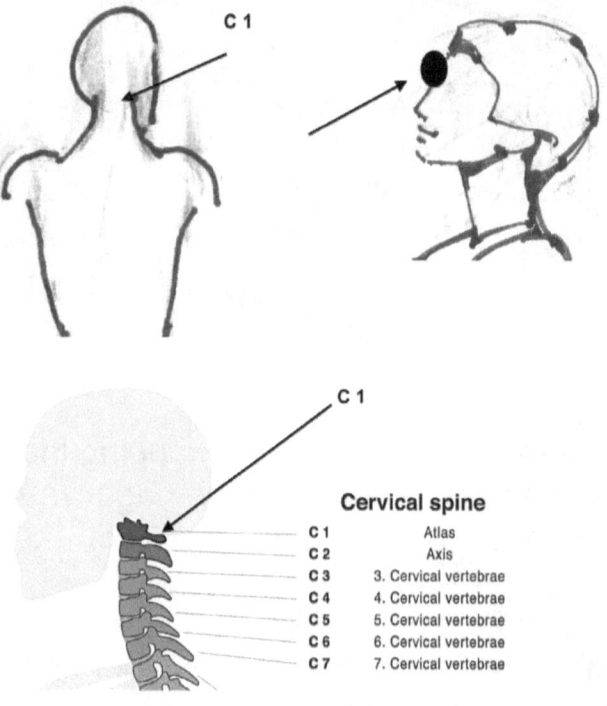

Switching

Most of the time I find the patient is just experiencing ordinary stressors of life. Perhaps an unexpected bill that comes due that you didn't know about, a personal conflict, a difficult business experience or something of that nature. That stress is more localized. It can also scramble the body, but not as seriously. I always check for that possibility as well, because it interferes with the accuracy of my muscle testing. There are three aspects to this method.

First Aspect

The person has to direct their gaze upwards towards their forehead while I test the muscle. If the muscle does not lock, they are switched. This is a minor switching, but enough to cause stress. To correct this state, rub (simultaneously on both sides) K 27 which is the acupuncture point where the clavicle meets the sternum and the navel, at the same time. Next, have them look up, retest the muscle, and it should lock. It is an indicator that the body is now back in focus.

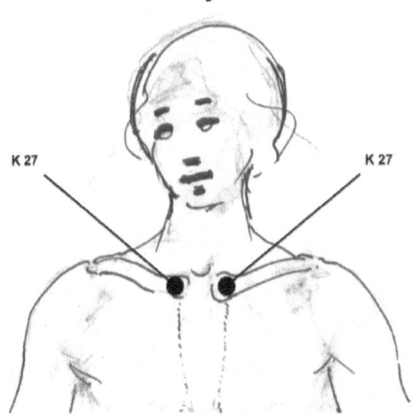

Second Aspect

The next step is testing for diaphragm tension. The diaphragm is a very emotionally oriented muscle, and when one is under a lot of emotional stress, it loses its tone.

Test

Gently push your fingertips underneath the bottom front rib to the right or left of the sternum, and test the muscle while your fingers are up in that spot. If it goes weak, that indicates that the diaphragm is weak. People will often state that when they have stress, they struggle to deeply inhale.

Treatment

To correct the diaphragm, rub down the full length of the sternum from the top to above the xiphoid process, which is the smallest part of the breastbone structure. You may feel sore and quite tender in that area.

Next, rub along the bottom rib on the <u>right side only</u> from the spine to the end at the side. These are what is called neuro-lymphatic reflexes - Chapman reflexes or points, which are an outward physical expression of internal muscular dysfunction. These reflexes are like a breaker switch system that relates to the lymphatic system. When they crash, the circuit goes off and that muscle ceases to function normally, because it is not getting sufficient amount of energy. These reflexes will be quite tender if they are overwhelmed and out of balance.
After this process, retest the muscle again, and now it should respond strong.

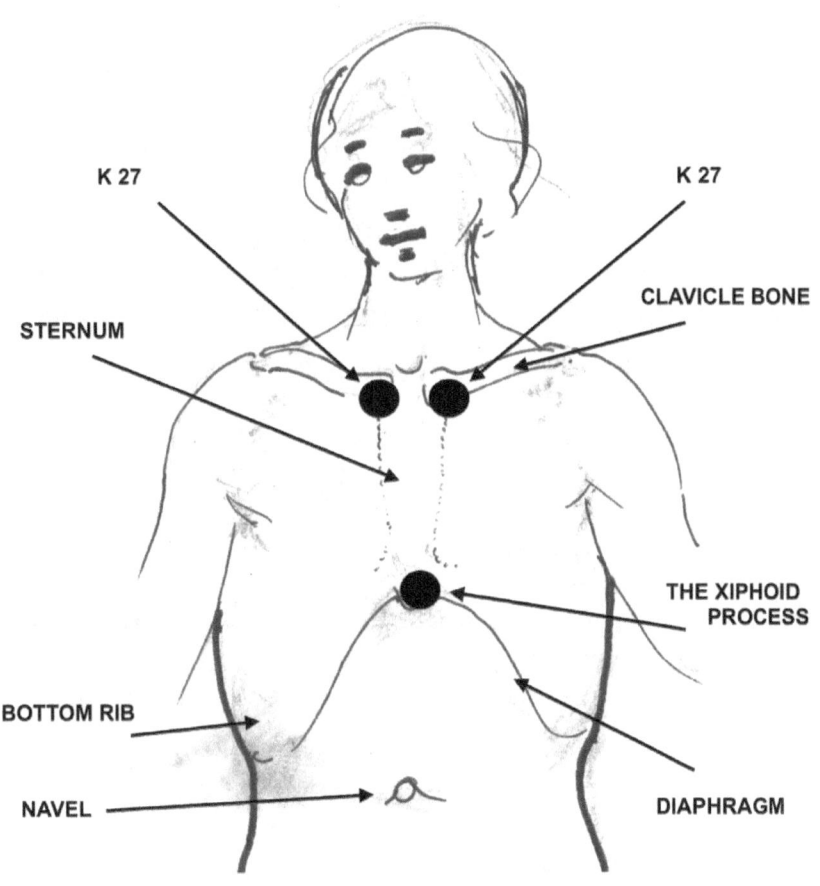

THE SWITCHING SYNDROME MAP

Third Aspect
The Ileocecal Valve Test

The ileocecal valve is a sphincter muscle situated at the junction of the ileum, which is the last portion of your small intestine, and the cecum, which is the first portion of your large intestine. It controls the flow of the small intestine contents into the large intestine, and vice versa. If it spasms open, the contents in the large intestine can back up into the small intestine and cause gassiness, bloating and pain.

If the spasm is closed, it is preventing the small intestine from emptying properly, which will cause similar uncomfortable side effects, gas, pain and indigestion. If the valve has been out for a longer period of time, it can also become the source of lower back pain. A person will also experience a general sense of pain over that specific area of intestines. Stress, liver dysfunction, excessive caffeine and raw foods are the main causes of ileocecal valve dysfunction. If you are experiencing a sudden onset of low back pain or gassiness, you can perform a self-test.

This can be accomplished by placing your fingers on the McBurney's Point, which is the area half way between the navel - bellybutton, and the top of the pelvis. Next, put gentle pressure down into the intestines and lightly move it up and down. It will probably feel sore which will indicate to the body, that it requires help.

To help with this issue, you can use the Ileocecal Valve Reset technique.

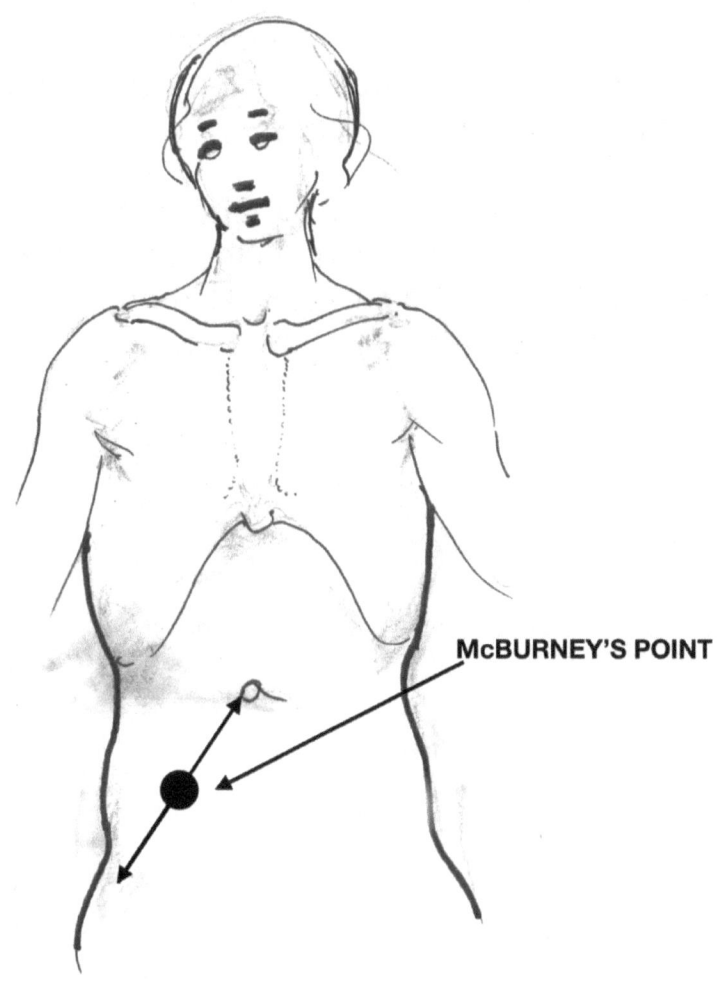

The McBurney's Point
The area halfway between the navel - bellybutton, and the top of the pelvis.

The Ileocecal Valve Reset

To reset the ileocecal valve, keep in mind the points will most likely feel quite tender and will require a fairly deep rubbing stroke. All the treatment points are on the right side of the body.

FIRST POINT

You will find the first point on the inside of the right heel, just slightly below the ankle bone. Find the point and firmly massage for a few seconds.

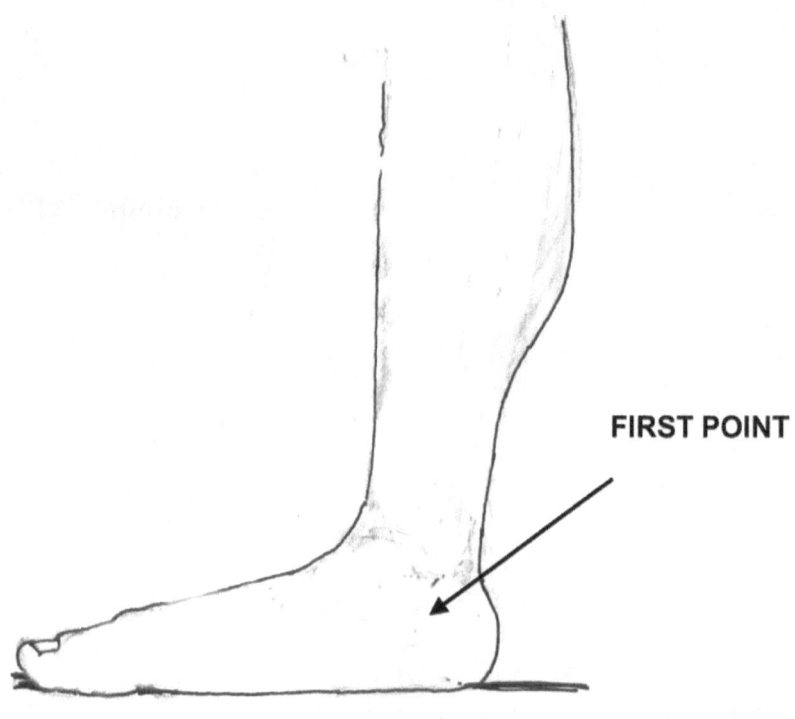

SECOND POINT

You will find the second point at the back of the calf muscle on the right side, just as calf begins to taper down to the lower part of the leg.

With firm pressure, go into the middle of that muscle and rub deeply. I find that point to be the most tender on almost everybody.

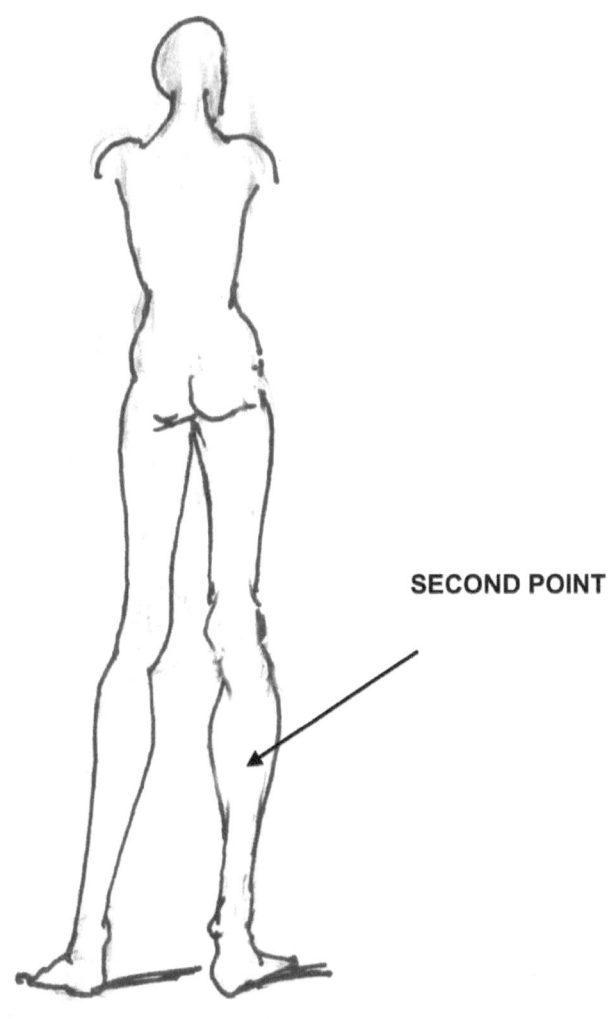

SECOND POINT

THIRD POINT

You will find the third point find at the top of the pelvis, which you used to find the McBurney's Point. Next, go over the outside edge of that and you will find an indentation there, and that is where you place your thumb and rub that point/spot.

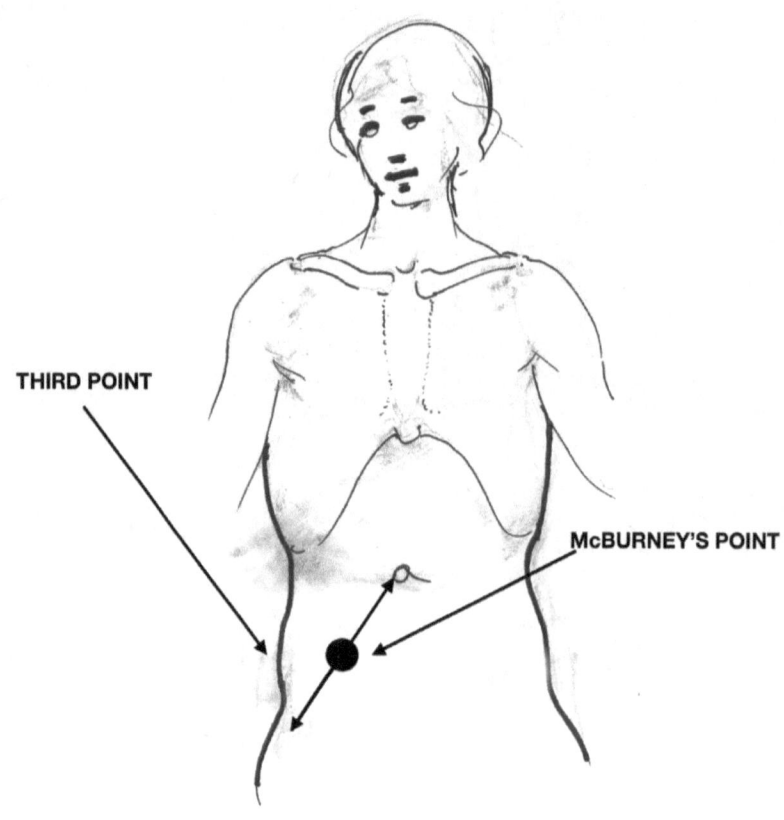

FOURTH POINT

You will find the fourth point on the front tip of the right shoulder and firmly rub that location.

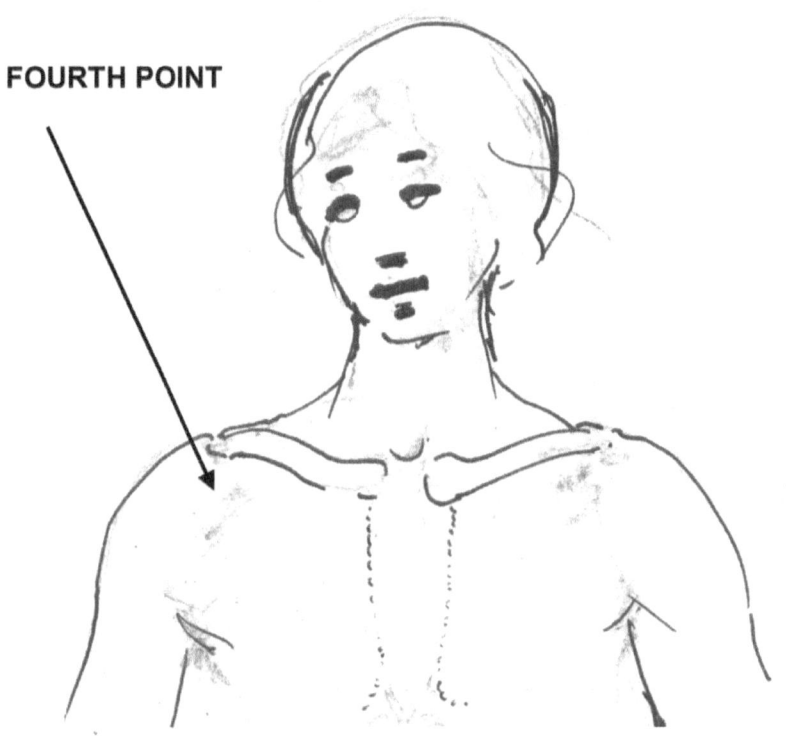

FIFTH POINT

You will find the fifth point at C3 - halfway between the bottom of the skull and the base of the neck, just off the spine into musculature to the right. This area will usually also be quite sore.

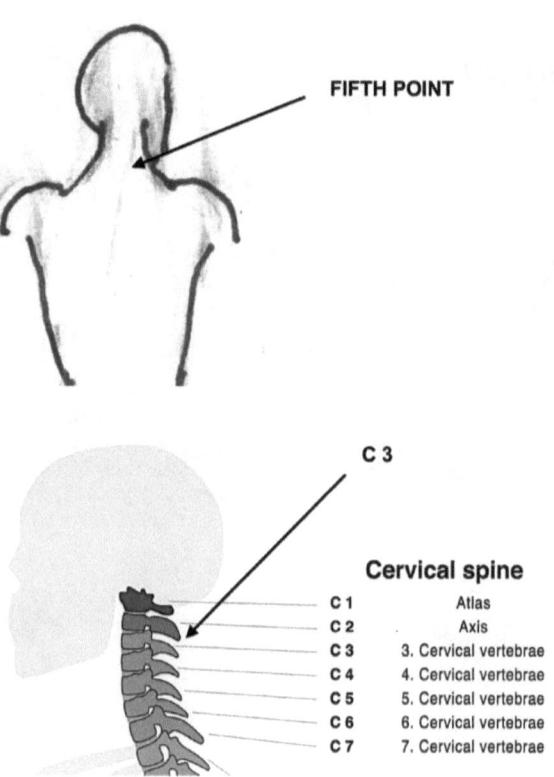

After this entire process, you place your fingers back to McBurney's Point, retest the muscle which should now give you a strong response.

Finding the Priority Organ

The body works on a priority system. Most of the people that seek my help have various metabolic problems. When a patient mentions they suffer from hormone imbalance or digestive issues, I check all those systems to find out which systems are dysfunctional. I use a reflex response for all organ and glandular systems to determine which one is the priority.

I may find five or six organs or gland systems that are out of balance, but there is always one that is the priority, and is affecting all the other glands and organs. Instead of giving my patients nutritional supplements to try to correct all these organs and glands, I choose to work on just the one priority. Once I succeed in improving the functioning of the priority organ, all the other organs and glands automatically shift into more balanced function, because they are no longer stressed by that one affected priority organ or gland that is a weak link.

When I find out where the balance is off, I begin communicating with the body to find the cause that is triggering this organ dysfunction. It can be mental, structural or emotional issues, candida, food allergies, heavy metals, virus or bacterial infection, fungus, parasites, or chemicals they are exposed to, or ingesting.
During the process, all organs and glands automatically shift into a more balanced function.

Working on the Priority Organ

The amount of time I spend working on the priority organ depends on how many areas of the body are challenged.
Once I find the priority, I explain to the patient:
"I will ask the body some questions and I just want you to keep holding your arm."

I go very silent, and commence with the process of mentally and emotionally completely connecting with the higher mental body of the patient.

Next, I begin asking questions:
"Please help me find the cause of this dysfunction for _____(the name of my patient).
Is this dysfunction caused by a mental or an emotional trigger?" It will respond with a yes or no.
"Is this caused by candida?"
It will respond with a yes or no.
"Is this caused by food allergies?"
It will respond with a yes or no.
"Is this caused by heavy metals?"
It will respond with a yes or no.
"Is this caused by Epstein Barr virus?"
It will respond with a yes or no.
"Is this caused by any other viruses or bacterial infections?"
It will respond with a yes or no.
"Is this caused by fungus or parasites?"
It will respond with a yes or no.
"Is this caused by a chemical in their environment

that they are reacting to?"
It will respond with a yes or no.
"Is this caused by a chemical they are ingesting, either nutritional or drug?"
It will respond with a yes or no.
"Is there a structural component?"
It will respond with a yes or no.
"Is there anything else that I have missed that is causing dysfunction in this organ?"
It will respond with a yes or no.

Next, I tabulate all the "Yes" answers and when it becomes clear and I determine that the cause is of emotional nature, I proceed to ask the body:
"Is it anger, fear, despair, grief or any other emotion that is involved?"
It usually comes up as anger, fear, despair, sometimes grief, if the patient has recently lost a loved one.
If the answer is anger, I go on in this direction and continue with the questions:
"Is this anger coming from their childhood?"
It will respond with a yes or no.
"Is it coming from an experience in life early on?"
It will respond with a yes or no.
"Is it coming from something that is happening currently?"
It will respond with a yes or no.
If the answer is "early childhood", I continue asking:
"Is there anything in your early childhood that caused you a lot of anger?"
Whatever the answer, I explain to the patient that we need to clear this unresolved residue of emotional

energy, because it is affecting the priority organ. I have a technique specifically designed for clearing that energy pattern.

If the source of challenges are food allergies, I will go though and check all the different foods, and see which ones the patient is reacting to.

If it is candida, I will place a vile of candida and check to see if that is the course of problem. I continue checking for fungus, parasites, food additives and so on.

The next step depends on the body's answers. During this process, I try to be as neutral as I can, and don't have any intentions as far as wanting anything to happen or wanting to have any information. I simply ask the body to tell me what is going on, so that I can effectively help it.

The body's answers are the result of muscle - testing technique and process. However, on occasion I hear a suggestion in my mind, and will pursue that.

For example: I may suddenly receive a message that I should ask a question about food additives. I will consider that suggestion and most likely the true source of challenge will be correctly revealed.
On the next visit, I will repeat the entire scan and occasionally the body will reveal another priority that needs to be corrected. I will continue working in this way until there are no more priorities and the patient has responded favorably.

A CASE STUDY PROCESS OF REVEALING THE PRIORITY ORGAN

I remember a patient who came to me because she was experiencing a lot of fatigue and anxiety. During the consultation she also expressed that' she had a very stressful job. I performed my usual scan of all the organs and glands, and I found the liver, adrenals, thyroid, small intestine and large intestine reflexes to be positive for dysfunction. I then had her therapy localize and put her hand on each one of the organ reflexes. Each one tested weak. She began with the liver reflex, which went weak. While she still held her hand on the liver reflex, I placed my finger on the adrenal reflex and when I retested her muscle, it kicked in. I told her that her body was letting us know, that her adrenals were affecting the liver. We repeated this process with every other organ and gland that was revealed during the scan, and in each case the adrenals corrected it. I knew at that point the adrenals were the priority.

Core Beliefs

Core beliefs are situated in our subconscious mind. Any negative life-beliefs and perceptions are basically our core beliefs. Various negative attitudes that we usually witness and pick up as children, result in basically governing our lives. As a direct consequence of succumbing to negative core beliefs, everything we do in our lives is usually geared around these difficult and limited negative feelings that we have about ourselves, while trying to compensate for them.

When I was growing up, they did not know what dyslexia was. I am dyslexic, and as a result, I am a bit of a slow reader. In grade school I was always placed in the slow reading classes. Unfortunately at that time, everyone in a slow reading class was automatically labeled dumb. I can vividly remember the teacher telling us that as a matter of fact, we were just not as smart as other kids. So I grew up thinking and believing that I was dumb and stupid. This deep-set conviction affected all my relationships with people. I simply did not feel comfortable and could not carry on a conversation or talk to anybody for a longer amount of time. I felt I had nothing to say, because I accepted the idea, that I was dumb and stupid. This perception negatively affected my business as well, because I simply didn't feel worthy of having a strong business.

Years later, when I attended a TBM seminar, I

discovered the core beliefs and this strong technique. So I said: "That is the most powerful technique I've seen!" I asked the teacher, if he would work with me.

He began the process by asking me:
"What is your core belief?"
I answered: "I believe that I am dumb and stupid."
And he continued:
"What kind of a person is dumb and stupid?"
And I replied: "Well, a loser."
He then declared:
"That is your core belief, that you are a loser!"
He proceeded with the step by step implementation of the technique on me, that quickly cleared that belief out of my subconscious mind. Once this initial step is accomplished, it results in a newly "void space" in your subconscious. It is most important that you focus on immediately filling and replacing that void with something positive.

The teacher gave me the following affirmation that I faithfully practiced for two months:
"I am smart and capable, and I deserve anything that the Universe can possibly give me. I can speak with anybody."

After two months of dedicated practice of the affirmation, I noticed that I could truly talk to anybody, it didn't matter how smart they were. I had patients that were PH.D's and physicists that are brilliant, I could talk to them on a normal and regular basis. My business practically doubled overnight, it was just absolutely amazing how my life changed. And I know

I am no Einstein, but it doesn't matter, because I accept myself now for who I am and what I can do.

CASE STUDY

I recently had a patient that I could see was struggling with a core belief going on in her system. We first worked on her fears and in the process of working with her, I heard this voice in my head that said: "Ask her about her core beliefs". And so I did.

She continuously stated: "Well, life is always hard." And I said: "What's behind that? There is a belief about yourself behind that."
She replied: "Oh yes, I know."
She understood what I was talking about, she just didn't know exactly what it was. So we had to go through some questioning to find out the source. And we worked on it for a while, and kept going further and deeper back into her past, until finally she exclaimed: "I am not worthy."
So I informed her: "That's your core belief."

We worked on that issue, and now she has an affirmation that she is absolutely worthy, and deserves everything wonderful that life has to offer her. It is really quite amazing how powerful these aspects can be for people. It was so fulfilling to see her on follow-up visits feeling much stronger and positive about herself and her health also really improved. It is essential to discover your core beliefs, as they hold the key to you removing self-imposed limitations that prevent you from living your life to the fullest potential.

Harmonization process

This technique was developed by TBM system founder, Dr. Victor Leon Frank DC,NMD, DO (1931-2010). I have been using his harmonization system for several years, because it seems to be such a key for so many problems. I use it to eliminate major challenging factors that are affecting many organs and glands.

If the cause is an emotional issue, then I will use the acupower treatment. If it is a core belief issue, then a different process is required. The harmonization is the technique I use to some degree every day on most everybody, especially because I often find the patient has underlying triggers, that can be eliminated by this process.

The harmonization process requires a fair amount of time. I have the patient hold the substance they are allergic to. If it's food allergies, I go through all different kinds of foods to find out which are the ones they are sensitive too. Next, I have them hold that substance, and I search out which organ or gland is registering that pattern. 99% of the time I find that the liver is where that pattern is locked up. In such a case, I will have them hold the liver reflex, while I adjust their spine in a certain sequence. This basically helps reprogram the body, so that the liver no longer reads that substance or frequency as being foreign, and something to react against.

That's where the harmonization comes in. It is an energetic frequency approach. That was one of the things that Dr.Victor Franks told me when I was studying with him in person.
I asked him:" What does it mean? You are harmonizing and desensitizing somebody to a virus or bacteria. Does that indicate that the virus or bacteria could destroy the body and the body would not know it's still present?"

And he said: "No. If the body stops reacting to it, then the virus has no effect on the body. And who cares if the virus is present, if it has no affect on the body? You're walking around with viruses in your body right now. If they are not affecting you, who cares?"

The harmonizing technique reprograms the body on a subtle frequency level. It's an energetic process.

Dr. Royal Raymond Rife (1888 – 1971) established that there is a frequency for every virus and bacteria. He found that if he could disturb that frequency in any way, it would basically kill the virus.

Harmonization is a similar process and works under comparable principles. We are harmonizing the body to the frequency of the virus, or whatever it is creating a disturbance within the body, and in doing so, we are upsetting that virus's frequency. As a result, it can no longer have an effect on anything else, and therefore it basically just dissolves and ceases to exist.

Reprograming the Spine

I use the spine and the nervous system to reprogram the body systems. Dr. Frank discovered through his technique, that there are certain areas of the spine that relate to different organs.

For instance, the liver is T2, T5 and T8. I don't adjust those spots on the spine, I have an arothrostim device and I begin at T2, T5 and then T8. I tap those spots on each side of the spine, and that stimulates the nerve supply to tell the liver to no longer react to that substance. I can only do three items at one time, since for some reason, the body won't accept more than three of a category.

Once I get through the three, then the process is to put them all together, and test them all together. That usually comes up weak, which means I have to reprogram that particular frequency. Next, we have a set of vials, and we use each one of those and reprogram each one. We have a blood vial, which is programed to the frequency of general blood, so we program that. Next, we program histamines.

Once we complete all this, we check for poison and toxicity. At the end I block them in a particular form, that basically helps the body register that new pattern into its "hard drive" sort of speak, and holds on to it and maintains it.
This is the basic technique that is taught by TBM.

My Addition for Advanced Reprograming

I have added another procedure to the process, which seems to give the patient longer lasting results. After completion of the process, I have the person sit up once again, and take all three items that I just harmonized them too.

Now I will proceed to go through all the different organs and glands, such as brain, throat, heart, lungs, liver, stomach, pancreas, as well as sinuses if pollen is the challenge, or various foods in case of food allergy.

At that point, I will ask the body which local area of the body this particular food or pollen is affecting. Each one that is confirmed, I proceed to harmonize it to that specific area. I found that when I do that, the whole mechanism holds much more effectively, and for a considerably longer period of time.

This is a direct result of my clearing the disturbance in that particular organ, as opposed to just the body in general. It is significantly more specific.

Ninety percent of this method is subtle energy work and meticulously triggering the nervous system to properly respond to that particular organ with which we are working.

My Protocol Guidelines

The following intricate steps describe the basics of my healing process and the foundation of my established multi-dimensional protocol.

STEP I. ~ ESTABLISH PATIENT DIMENSION
I begin by silently asking the patient's body:
"Are you in this dimension?" If the muscle test response is negative, I continue with questions:
'What dimension are you in?"
And I begin counting: one and I test, two and so on. When I reach the number that accurately signals which dimension the body is in, the arm will respond strongly. I carry on.
"Are you in the 6th dimension?"
The body will confirm and respond with a "Yes."
Now I ask the body to take me to the 6th dimension. I simply stand there and silently count; one, two, three and so on.

I sense a powerful flush of energy that goes through my body with each dimension. When I say ONE, I sense a flush of energy, and continue TWO and get another flush of energy. I proceed until I get to the dimension that the body is in, in this case the 6th. Now I sense an immense flush of energy that feels different, and actually remains sustained.
Now I ask the body: "Am I in the 6th dimension?"
The body responds with a YES or NO.
Once I am in the same dimension as my patient, I begin checking for stress switches.

Being in the same dimension as my patient seems to unveil things that I wouldn't discover otherwise. It plays a crucial role and is of great importance in helping me uncover the correct information.

If I am not in the same dimension as my patient, the answers won't show up on the patient's body in this dimension. This aspect of the technique has been crucially important for me, because not being dimensionally aligned with my patient would prevent me from registering their true stress levels. I could go though all my reflexes to find all the dysfunctional organs and still not get a clear picture of what's truly going on with the body. I would receive just a very limited view. My method of establishing a multi-dimensional presence is crucial in proper patient assessment.

STEP II. ~ POLARITY

The next step is to check for accurate polarity. If that happens to read as incorrect, the patient is not testable to begin with. To check the polarity, you put the tip of your finger on the bridge of the nose and test the muscle. If the response is weak, the polarity is correct for testing.

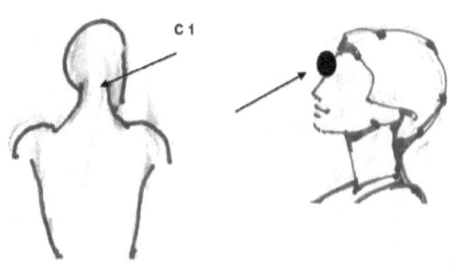

STEP III. ~ PSYCHOLOGICAL REVERSAL

Next, I check the patient for psychological reversal. They place their hand on top of their head, palm down. It should be strong. If the indication is reversed, such as weak when the palm is down and strong when the back of the hand is on top of their head and palm is up, then that indicates they are psychologically reversed and it means that somewhere along the way they have been through extreme stress and it has really scrambled their energy.

To correct this condition, I have them tap the little finger's side of the hand, and repeat the affirmation:
**"I deeply accept myself
even though I feel miserable."**
This affirmation needs to be repeated out loud three times. It does not matter which hand is used in this exercise. Next, I recheck to see if it has switched back to being strong with the palm down and weak with the palm up.

STEP IV. ~ STRESS SWITCH

Next, I do a general kind of stress switch. The correction for stress switching is as following:
Rub the navel and K27 clockwise at the same time for a few seconds. Retest again.

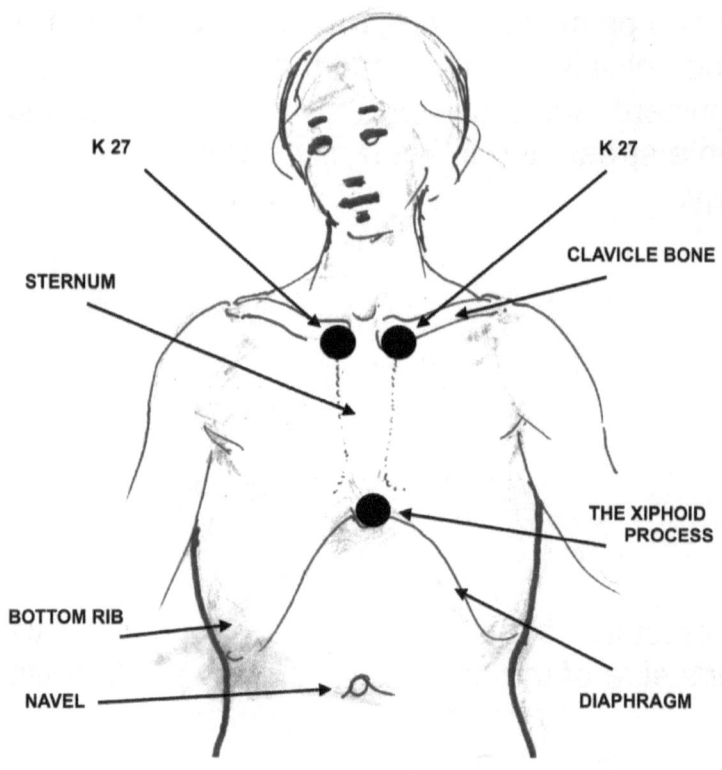

STEP V. ~ DIAPHRAGM

I check the diaphragm by taking my fingertips and gently placing them underneath the rib, just adjacent to the end of the sternum, just off to the right or left side. Test the muscle again. To correct, rub down the full length of the sternum, and along the base of the 12th rib, on the right side only.

STEP VI. ~ ILEOCECAL VALVE

Next step is to find McBurney's point which is halfway between the navel and the anterior part of the illium. Retest the muscle.

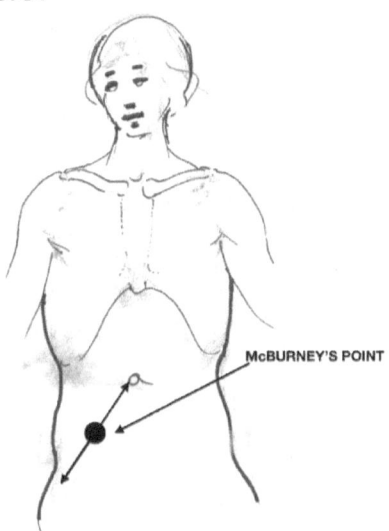

ILEOCECAL VALVE CORRECTION

Gently rub the points along the entire right side of the body. 1. Inside of the right heal below the ankle 2. right calf muscle, 3. the illium, 4. front tip right shoulder, 5. C3 on the right. Retest the ileocecal valve.

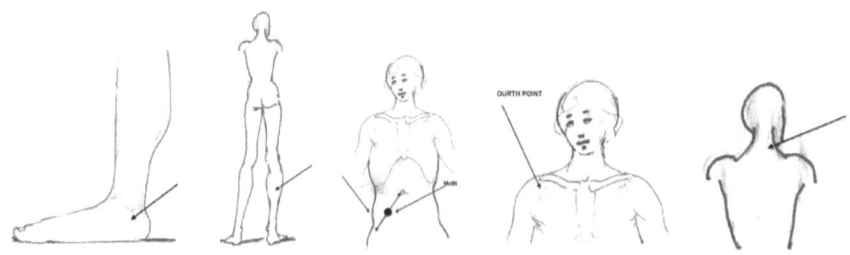

STEP VI. ~ THE BASICS

This is a test for dehydration and which case you test the right psoas muscle (the **psoas muscle** is located in the lower lumbar region of the spine and extends through the pelvis to the femur.) If that is weak you have to suspect that the patient is dehydrated. However, sometimes the psoas muscle can be simply weak from stress and the person may not be dehydrated. So I use another reflex for dehydration, where you place your finger right at the tip of the nose and check the muscle. If the response is weak along with the psoas muscle, then dehydration is certain.

STEP VII. ~ CHECK THE SUGAR BALANCE

Next step is to check the body's ability to balance the sugar. Bend the right leg and lift the left leg while straight. Push down on the left leg, and it should be solid. Bend the left leg and raise the right leg while straight and should be strong also.

STEP VIII. ~ CHECK THE BACTERIAL INFECTION

Next I will check for either bacterial or virus infections. I found that the reflex where you hook your fingers over the top of the left clavicle and test the muscle - that's a good reflex for someone that's having a sinus or lung infection. It seems to correlate with strep pneumonae. There is a virus reflex on both sides of the body between the 7th and 8th rib. I place several fingers over that area and test the muscle. If that comes up, it indicates the person may have a virus. I can offer the patient nutritional supplements for that as well.

STEP IX. ~ CHECK THE REFLEXES

Now the body is ready to be tested for dysfunction. If you don't prepare the body to be tested, you can't treat the symptoms. If a patient is in another dimension, or stressed out, they are energetically scrambled and can't respond or be receptive.
I do my best to unscramble the body and get it to the point where I can actually get the correct answers.

At that point I go through my reflex sequence. I check the liver, then gallbladder, the adrenals, the heart, the thyroid, the pituitary, the hypothalamus, the stomach, the head of the pancreas, the pancreas, the body of the pancreas, the spleen, small intestine, the large intestine and the kidneys.

Then I keep a mental note of all organs and glands that went weak and write them down. I explain to the patient what I just found.

STEP X. ~ FIND THE PRIORITY

Next, I inform the patient that I will look for and focus on the priority. I have the patient what they call "therapy localize" by placing their hand on the organ reflex for each organ or gland, that was positive during my scan. For instance: the person places their hand on the liver reflex which will still be weak, and I contact the adrenal reflex and the muscle locks in, and I know the adrenals are affecting the liver. I will ask the patient if they felt the difference and explain what it meant.

Next I go and check all the other organs and see if

the adrenals are affecting any other organs or glands. Let's say we find liver, adrenals, thyroid, small intestine or large intestine. I will have the patient do therapy localization for the thyroid, and then I will check the adrenals. If the adrenals are the priority, then the thyroid reflex will also strengthen.

Next step is to have the patient place their hand on small intestine reflex and that will go weak. I will then put my hand on the adrenal reflex, and if the adrenals are affecting the small intestine that will strengthen it. We will continue with the same principle on the large intestine all the different parts of intestine, and do the adrenals and it will always strengthen the large intestine reflex if that is indeed the priority.

STEP XI. ~ DIALOGUE WITH THE BODY

Once I find the priority, I write it down and tell the patient:
"I want you to keep holding your arm, and I will ask your body some questions."
I then proceed to do this process in silence, because I don't want the person's mind interfering with the test in any way. If the adrenals are the priority, I will be testing the muscle and have my fingers on the adrenals if I received a weak muscle response.

I always ask the person's higher mental body to assist me in helping them find out what is causing the adrenal dysfunction.
My first dialogue goes as follows:
"Higher mental body of Leslie, please show me what is causing this adrenal dysfunction."

This is a way for me to connect with the body. Then the body responds. I go ahead and begin asking my questions. If the answer is YES, then that question is affecting the adrenals.

The first question that I ask is:
"Is this a mental or emotional disorder?"
It will respond with a Yes or No.
If the answer is YES, I continue.
"What kind of emotion is involved? Is it anger, fear, despair, grief?"
I inquire for each emotion separately.
It will respond which emotion it is, sometimes two or three, anger, grief and despair.
My next question will zero-in further:
"When did this occur? Is this a childhood emotion?"
If the answer is YES, then I know that it is something that happened in early childhood that caused that emotion to be deeply imprinted in the body.
If the answer is NO, then I will inquire further:
"Was it a situation that happened recently, a few years ago?"
It will respond with a Yes or No. I try to hone in to when that emotion happened, and once I determine that aspect, I keep the answer in the back my mind, while proceeding further.
My next inquiry explores more specifics:
"Is there candida involved?"
It will respond with a Yes or No.
"Are there food allergies?"
It will respond with a Yes or No.
"Is it pollen allergies?"
It will respond with a Yes or No.

Pollen allergies do not affect the organs as much.
My questions continue:
"Are there any heavy metals?
"Is there Epstein Barr virus or Cytomegly virus?"
"Are there any other viruses or bacteria affecting this patient? Any fungus or parasites?
Chemicals in environment? Chemicals that they are ingesting that area affecting them?
Food additives? Lyme disease?
Are there any antibiotics affecting the body?(especially if they have just had surgery or an infection. Is there any mold?"

I write down the YES answers and then I will deepen my investigation about each positive response I find and begin asking the body more thoroughly. For instance, if I found emotions of anger from their early childhood, I will ask them:
"Is there anything in your childhood that caused you a lot of anger?"
Most people will reveal a problematic parent or a similar predicament that happened in their early childhood. It will make a lot of sense in that respect. Sometimes a person can't remember anything at all. I suggest they think about it and we will check on it next time.

Usually, by the next visit they will have remembered a past situation in question. This observation is very seldom wrong. We talk about it, and mention that we will resolve this challenging issue at a different time, when I will use the Acupower technique that helps erase traces of old unwanted and negative emotional scars.

If the challenging source is something else, like for example candida, I have a vile for candida which I will place on their body and see if it goes weak, which it usually does.

I will inquire further and ask:

"Do you have a tendency to crave carbs or sweets?" And they almost always confirm.

If the source of challenges are food allergies, then I have a list of vials of food allergies, and several other kinds of foods with which I can muscle test them.

I list the responses on their chart.

I also have a whole collection set of vials for various heavy metals that I will place on the body and muscle test. If the response is weak, I work with the patient in narrowing down the answers.

Usually if I am suspecting something, I will simply make that part of my questioning procedure. In case of fungus and parasites I will use thorough muscle testing with vials relating to them.

Chemicals in the environment present another common issue, and in that case I ask the body to be more specific such as: are these chemicals found in cleaning products, or related to painting in case of artists, who spend a lot of time surrounded by art supplies. I also ask about cosmetics, perfumes, laundry detergent, or perhaps fumes from fresh paint they use on a daily basis.

I also inquire about any vitamins, drugs or chemicals they are ingesting. Oftentimes the over the counter vitamins are not the best quality.

On their next visit I often ask the patient to bring with them whatever they are consuming, so we can test the body and see if it is a good match, and I can harmonize them to that if necessary.

Once I get through all these thorough steps, at the very end, I'll ask the patient's body the following: "Do you need any nutritional supplemental support to get stronger?"
Usually the body will respond with a solid YES and I will then ask the body to select different nutritional supplements.

Most importantly, once I have released all the triggers, the patient is already feeling better.

My approach is to provide nutritional supplements only for a short term use, to help the body rebuild the organ or gland in question, until it can stand on their own.

The full recovery time depends on the patient's overall health, lifestyle, eating habits, stress levels, and individual physical weakness or strength.

III.
Heal your body

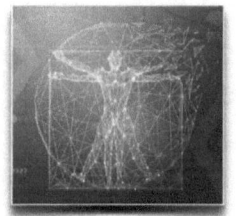

Self~Testing Technique

There are several ways that you can self-test and you just need to explore and find a way with which you feel most comfortable.
A good method is using the thumb and the little finger. Press them tightly together and then by using the other hand, try to separate them. You will detect if those muscles are strong or weak. This approach doesn't appeal to me much.
Some people raise the leg and push down on the leg and test themselves that way.

I prefer the pendulum effect. At first when I began using it, I felt I needed to clearly establish what is a YES and what is a NO answer.

Then I stood neutral to see which way it would lean. If I went forward it was YES, leaning backwards is a NO. This is the method I've been using ever since.

When I was in a health food store, I wanted to test nutritional supplements. I held them to my chest and asked my body, if this nutrition is going to benefit me. It is important to completely clear my mind when I ask a question.

The Ten Golden Rules that I Follow

When a patient is describing various challenging symptoms that are connected to their illness, I follow these rules that help me to quickly establish the underlying cause of their discomfort.

I. Anxiety

I always check the adrenals for anybody that comes to me with anxiety issues. That is an absolute given. Adrenals can also be connected to type 2 diabetes, since they help balance the sugar in the body. The pancreas produces the insulin, but it is the adrenals that regulate and maintain the balance and use of insulin.

II. Sudden drop in Energy

A sudden drop in energy almost always points to an onset of a virus. If you struggle getting up in the morning and feel tired, a virus might be coming on. By taking a remedy at this crucial point, you will usually prevent or minimize the effects of the virus, limiting it to a 24 hour period. Natural supplements are most helpful for this purpose.

III. Checking for psychological reversal, switching and dimension

Before starting my evaluation, especially if the person has been to several other doctors and has not seen any positive results, I always check for psychological reversal, switching and the possibility of patient's "functioning" on a different dimension. It is of essential importance that I can energetically reach the patient and communicate with their body properly.

IV. Diarrhea, Constipation or Depression

If a patient complains of diarrhea, constipation or depressions, I always check the liver first. Adrenals can also cause these symptoms, but throughout all my years of experience, I found that most of the time, the liver controls that aspect. If I can get the liver working, these issues rapidly improve and dissipate.

V. Chronic neck pain

If a person suffers of chronic neck pain that is not a direct result of an injury, I first need to determine how inflamed and painful the affected area is, in order to assess how much I can work on it. I like to have the tissues healed to some degree.

With **motion palpation** technique we learned that a joint can be locked up in a forward position so you have to adjust from front to the back. I find this to be really common with C1.

If someone suffers from chronic neck pain, then C1 is almost always locked up. This is especially detectable by having the patient turn their head to the right and left shoulder, while you palpate C1. It should rotate posterior when the head is turned in both directions. If it does not to one side and the rotation is limited on that side, then it is anteriorly fixated, and needs to be adjusted posteriorly. The improvement after a proper adjustment is instant and very effective.

VI. Ankle or knee pain

If a person has ankle or knee pain, or suffers from Plantar fasciitis, which is the inflammation of a thick band of tissue connecting the heel bone to the toes, I always check the cuboid bone on that side of the ankle. The **cuboid bone** is one of the seven tarsal **bones** located on the lateral (outer) side of the foot. If the condition is worse when the patient is walking, it is most likely caused by a locked up cuboid bone. Once adjusted, the patient feels immediate relief. The tarsal bones and the ankle are responsible for absorbing all the stress every time you take a step. When the cuboid is locked, the stress can't be absorbed and is transferred to other tissues, either the foot, knee or even hip, which results in lower back problems. This challenge can be accelerated if you have the habit of sitting cross legged with the ankle turned in, for a long periods of time, which causes a locked up cuboid. It is important to be mindful of how you place your feet while in sitting position.

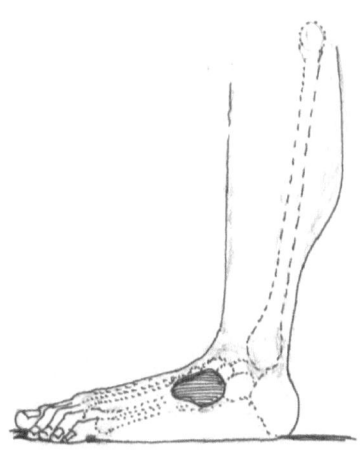

THE CUBOID BONE

VII. Knee pain

If a patient is complaining of constant pain in their knee, even when they are not walking, I check the liver and the popliteus muscle. This is the little short muscle on the knee joint that crosses the back of the knee. It is one of the major knee stabilizers. Because this muscle is closely related to the gallbladder meridian it is also associated with liver dysfunction and may as a consequence "blow out". If someone is suffering from knee pain, specially after a recent fall, then I will always also examine the patilla - kneecap bone.

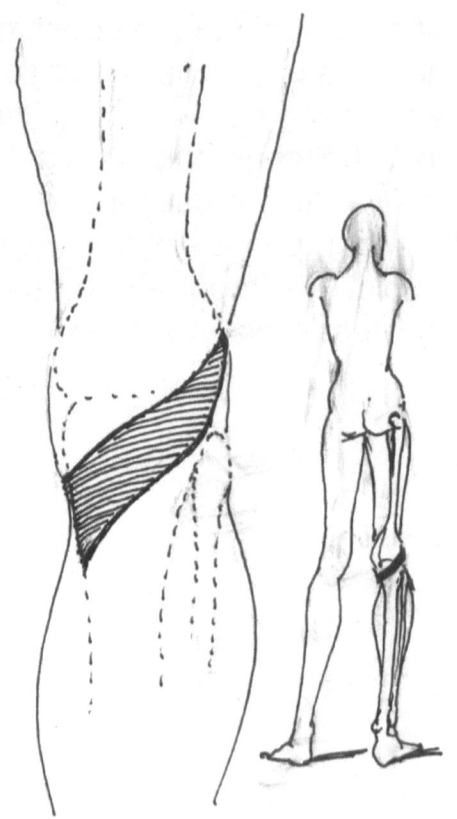

THE POPLITEUS MUSCLE

VIII. Chronic cough

When a patient comes to me with a chronic cough and it is not a bacterial or viral infection, it is most likely an allergy or fungal infection. I had a case of a patient with chronic cough that had a fungal infection. In my experience a fungal infection is most often the root cause of chronic, long standing cough.

IX. Infertility

If a patient is experiencing infertility or period issues, I always check pituitary. I have successfully helped numerous patients who have enjoyed healthy pregnancies after receiving pituitary work. Often these patients had previously been to fertility clinics, to no avail. I find that if the pituitary is working properly, the woman is more balanced and the chances of successful pregnancy are considerably higher. In some cases where patients suffered from a previous miscarriage and were quite fearful that another pregnancy may result in a loss, once the pituitary was adjusted they enjoyed a problem free full term pregnancy and delivered a healthy baby. The main cause of setting pituitary gland off balance, is stress. Cranial adjustment and proper nutritional supplements will help strengthen the pituitary. A weak pituitary can be hereditary. I have had cases of inherited weakness in pituitary, where the mother of the patient also suffered from painful and heavy irregular periods. In such cases, it will take a bit more time to regain the strength and balance of the pituitary and increase fertility.

X. Chronic low back pain

In case of chronic low back pain, I always examine the spine, but I also check the liver function and the Quadratus lumborum muscle. I learned this years ago involving trigger point therapy developed by Janet G.Travell, MD.

The Quadratus lumborum is a flat muscle that attaches to the bottom of the ribs and the top of the pelvis, on both sides of the body. It is used a lot when you are sitting, which causes the muscle to get very tight. Usually one is not aware of this, until they move about, or bend over to pick something up. All of a sudden they have the onset of chronic pain either in the lower back or in their groin.

If the pain does not go below the knee, it indicates that it's muscular oriented. If it descends below the knee and into the foot, then the cause is almost always neurological. In this case, we observe the pain expanding through the glute muscle down the front or back of the leg, and up the back. This can be caused by prolonged sitting or engaging in intense manual labor.

The challenge in correctly addressing this issue presents itself because the pain is not necessarily felt in that region, but in other areas. When you properly address the Quadratus lumborum muscle by pushing on it to release the trigger points, the patient will experience an intense and very helpful adjustment.

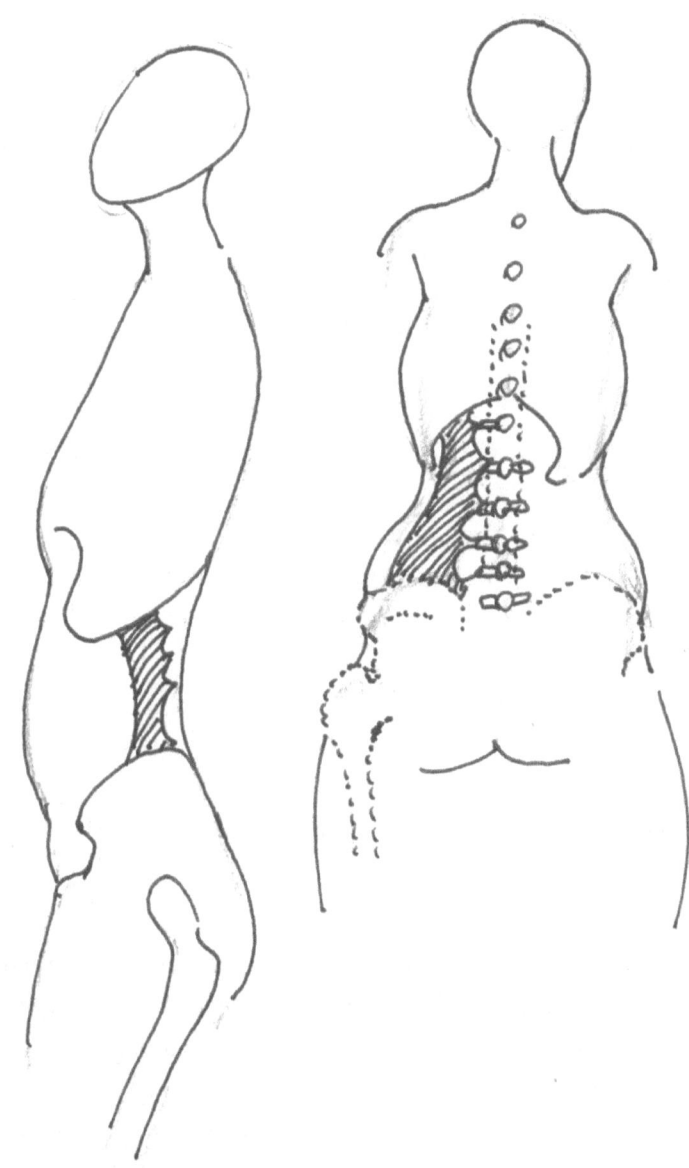

THE QUADRATUS LUMBORUM MUSCLE

The Five Golden Rules I share with my Patients

Every successful healing process requires your conscious and disciplined participation. These five golden rules are my recommendations for ongoing self-care, while cultivating a healthy lifestyle to help expedite your body's natural restorative process.

I. Virus

If you are fighting off a virus, I insist you allow for sufficient rest, so your body can properly recover. Find a way to make it possible to remain in bed and do nothing for the day. Take nutritional supplements and obey to strict fulltime rest. This way you will be able to recover in a day.

II. Candida

If you are trying to fend off candida, I suggest you double the intake of probiotics for at least a week. The intestinal microbiom is the only way your body can keep candida under control. Make sure you take probiotics every day for 4 months. Follow up with 2 or 3 times a week maintenance regimen to help restore and rebuild your microbiom. This is essential for a better immune system and healthy brain function.
A strong sign that you have candida is when you have extreme craving for sweets. Keep in mind, that consuming probiotic yogurt is simply not enough to remedy and regain balance in acute cases of candida, however, it is excellent for ongoing maintenance.

III. Hiatal Hernia

If you are suffering from the acid reflux, the following tip will be of great help for you. I almost always find the presence of the acid reflex when someone has a hiatal hernia. They usually spend months taking the acid reflux medications, however once the hiatal hernia is adjusted, the improvement is immediate. My first piece of advice for you is that while you're eating, sit with a very straight back. By eating while sitting on a soft couch, or in the car, you will most likely push your full stomach upwards and it will get stuck again. If you pick up something on a full stomach while not bending your knees, it can also cause the hernia to return.

Test

Press in and gently up under the xiphoid process while testing the arm muscle. If the muscle weakens, it indicates the condition of hiatal hernia.

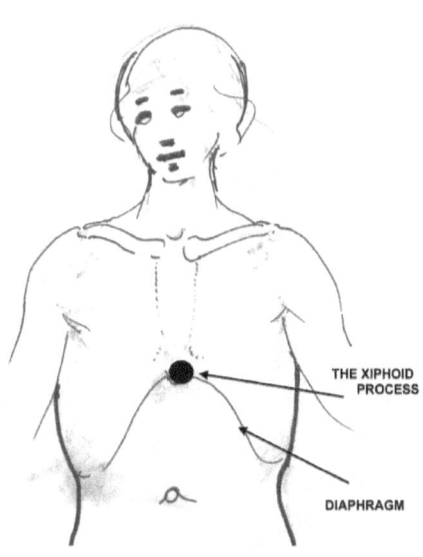

Treatment

An easy option is to drink a quart of water on an empty stomach and jump up and down several times. The weight of the water will usually help release the hiatal hernia, unless it is severe. There is also a physical adjustment procedure that can and should only be performed by an experienced professional practitioner.

IV. Gratitude

Above all, your personal disposition towards life in general, plays an incredibly important role in your state of overall health. Keep in mind that stress is the enemy, while inner peace is your greatest asset. Living in the moment and recognize all the everyday blessings you may be taking for granted. How can you recognize and appreciate all the gifts the Universe offers? Practice gratitude. Consciously awaken your inner awareness, your ability to observe and accept the gift of your healthy body and mind. Cultivate a positive attitude and always practice gratitude.

V. Healing

While the world around us is in a constant state of hurry, we unfortunately adopt the same habit and allow it to rule our lives. Your relationship with your body requires the basics of proper self-care and patience. When you are undergoing any kind of a treatment or healing process, your body needs proper rest and care in order to effectively recover. Always give your body much patience and a generous amount of time to allow healing. It will thank you and reward you.

Questionnaire

Circle the number which best describes the intensity of your symptoms.

0 - NONE   1 - MILD   2 - MODERATE   3 - SEVERE

SECTION A

1. Fullness for extended time after meals	0 1 2 3
2. Bloating	0 1 2 3
3. Lower Bowel Gas	0 1 2 3
4. Stomach Pains just before or after meals	0 1 2 3
5. Dependecy on Antiacids	0 1 2 3
6. Fatigue and sleepiness after eating	0 1 2 3
7. Feeling weak and shaky	0 1 2 3
8. Nose bleeds	0 1 2 3
9. Heartburn after eating	0 1 2 3
10. Painful stomach or intestine	0 1 2 3
11. Chronic Lung Congestion	0 1 2 3
12. Skin Rashes	0 1 2 3
13. Numbness in Extremities	0 1 2 3
14. Vertigo	0 1 2 3
15. Craving sweets	0 1 2 3
16. Poor memory	0 1 2 3
17. Crave sweets with no relief	0 1 2 3
18. Increased Anger and frequent outbursts	0 1 2 3
19. Low Back pain	0 1 2 3
20. Vaginal itching	0 1 2 3
21. Leg Cramps or restless legs at night	0 1 2 3
22. Water Retention	0 1 2 3

SECTION B

1. History and Constipation   0 1 2 3
2. Alternating Constipation and Diarrhea 0 1 2 3
3. Headaches   0 1 2 3
4. Depressed / apathetic   0 1 2 3
5. Chronic Pain especially in the Lower Back 0 1 2 3
6. Skin Rashes   0 1 2 3

SECTION C

1. Chronic fatigue   0 1 2 3
2. Dizziness upon standing   0 1 2 3
3. Headaches   0 1 2 3
4. Eye sensitive to bright Light   0 1 2 3
5. Entire body aches /painful to touch   0 1 2 3
6. Chronic Pain especially in Joints   0 1 2 3
7. Fibromyalgia   0 1 2 3
8. Poor concentration/Brain Fog   0 1 2 3
9. Vertigo   0 1 2 3
10. Water retention   0 1 2 3
11. Nervousness / Anxiety   0 1 2 3
12. Wake up mid-night, can't fall back to sleep 0 1 2 3

SECTION D

1. High Blood Cholesterol   0 1 2 3
2. Swollen /Bulging eyes   0 1 2 3
3. Sensitive to Cold   0 1 2 3
4. Chronic Fatigue   0 1 2 3
5. Fibromyalgia   0 1 2 3
6. Hair loss   0 1 2 3

7. Thinning or loss of outside 1/3 of eyebrows	0 1 2 3
8. Gain weight easily	0 1 2 3
9. Poor concentration / Brain fog	0 1 2 3
10. Poor memory	0 1 2 3
11. Tender Breasts	0 1 2 3

SECTION E

1. Premenstrual Tension	0 1 2 3
2. Infertility	0 1 2 3
3. Irregular periods	0 1 2 3
4. Over 15 years of age, not begin period	0 1 2 3
5. Miscarriages	0 1 2 3
6. Heavy menstrual bleeding and/or cramping	0 1 2 3
7. Hot Flashes	0 1 2 3

SECTION F

1. Chronic fatigue	0 1 2 3
2. Poor concentration	0 1 2 3
3. Headaches	0 1 2 3
4. Entire Body aches - painful to Touch	0 1 2 3
5. Chronic Pain	0 1 2 3
6. Bulls-eye Rash after a tick bite	0 1 2 3
7. Flu like symptoms	0 1 2 3
8. Paralysis on one side of the Face	0 1 2 3
9. Night Sweats and Chills	0 1 2 3

Keys

SECTION A

Miscellaneous - any number 2 or greater
Questions
1. Hiatal Hernia / Low Hydrochloric Acid
2. Hiatal Hernia / Low Hydrochloric Acid
3. Ileocecal Valve Syndrome / Low Hydrochloric Acid
4. Hiatal Hernia / Low Hydrochloric Acid
5. Hiatal Hernia / Low Hydrochloric Acid
6. Food Allergies
7. Hypoglycemic (Low Blood Sugar) Attack
8. Calcium Lactate (Standard process) will help
9. Hiatal Hernia / Low Hydrochloric Acid
10. Hiatal Hernia / Low Hydrochloric Acid
11. Bacterial / Virus infection, Fungus
12. Fungus, Candida, Food and Food additives Allergy
13. Diabetes, Neurological ~ spine, Muscle Trigger Points
14. Upper Cervical, Ear ossicles, Adrenals
15. Candida
16. Heavy metals, Thyroid
17. Candida
18. Low Magnesium
19. Spinal, Muscle Trigger points, Liver
20. Candida
21. Low calcium, Low Magnesium, B12 / Folic Acid
22. Water Utilization (use TBM technique)

SECTION B
Total Points 12 or over
Liver should be evaluated

SECTION C
Total Points 24 or over
Adrenals should be evaluated

SECTION D
Total Points 22 or over
Thyroid should be evaluated

SECTION E
Total Points 14 or over
Pituitary should be evaluated

SECTION F
Total Points 18 or over
Lyme Disease should be evaluated

The Universal Presence

GOD & DIVINITY

Each one of us has a very personal and unique relationship with the Higher Power, Universe or God. In my work with patients, I often ask to be granted the information needed to help me find and determine the patient's problem, so I can help eliminate their suffering and discomfort.
In particularly challenging cases, I always call on the God ~ Power with a silent request:
"Please tell me what I need to do in order to help this person the best way I possibly can."

It is interesting, because sometimes I don't get any answers, but then suddenly the patient will say something that is precisely what I need to hear. It assists in guiding me to help them improve. Quite often this information is revealed in mysterious ways since it actually comes through the patient, and not just through me.

My philosophy is that no one is a healer. God is the only healer that works through the person's body. I consider myself strictly a facilitator. I help the body by removing whatever triggers I can find, that are causing that body to use extra energy while trying to survive. Once I help correct those complex situations, the body regains the energy and ability to function in a more normal and balanced way. Then it can heal itself.

My approach is to completely remove myself out of the situation and just ask for God's help in showing me what action is necessary to help this person. And then I do not push further, I just simply let it go. I don't try to think things through any more than necessary.

I clear my mind, and enter a state of focused receptivity, while I begin working though necessary steps, that simply just came to my mind. I examine and check various aspects of the patient. It is as if an invisible force triggers and guides me as I engage in the therapeutic process. I simply know the next best step and proceed without doubt.

I believe each individual has a choice, how to establish their relationship with this omnipresence. Whatever path they choose, perhaps through meditation, prayer, or religious practice, it is up to them.

My personal practice is to spend an hour every morning connecting with God. I call it *my grateful period*, where I just tell God how grateful I am for all the blessing I have, all the abundance I need, and all the patients I meet. During that time, I ask God how can I be of utmost service to my patients. I speak from my heart, thanking God in deep gratitude.

I believe that practicing gratitude is absolutely paramount. I don't pray because I believe praying is asking God for something, while all the time expecting something more. And to me, everything is already there.

If God wants us to have it, it's there. I say I am grateful for the abundance that comes in, even if I don't seem to have it right at that moment, and then it just shows up.

To me faith is really important. It is primary in one's life, especially concerning one's health. By cultivating gratitude for the past, the present and all our future needs, we step into alignment and receptivity with God's spectacular ability to provide for us everything we'll ever need or desire. If you carry deep faith and are gifted with an abundance of health, your life is extraordinarily beautiful.

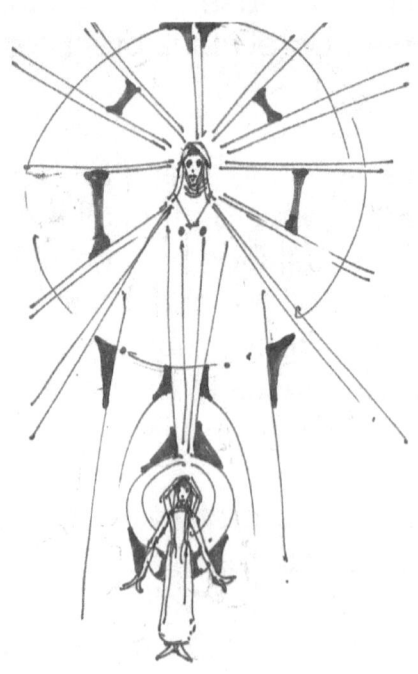

Final Thoughts

I am sure there are many practitioners who, like me, have been listening to their patients throughout the years and learned information of how the body functions and interacts with itself. I have found that the subtle triggers the body is reacting to oftentimes do not even create the symptoms one would expect, like a food allergy upsetting the intestines. As an example, many times I have found a food allergy that is affecting an organ function but the patient's symptoms do not seem to be related to the food allergy. I therefore have grown to respect the body's ability to interact with itself in order to try and maintain balance. Due to this subtle interaction, I see the body as a miracle in its ability to adapt to its environment. I know there are a lot of people who are suffering many types of diseases, but to me, as toxic as our general environment has become, it is quite a wonder that anyone survives.

My goal in the last 35 years of being in practice has always been to attempt to improve my patients' ability to adapt to whatever environment they are in so that they can live their lives as free from physical problems as possible.

I have personally experienced my own periods of trauma with seven and a half years of chemotherapy, alternative therapies and radiation for throat cancer (squaemous cell carcinoma). Even though the alternative therapies were unable to alleviate the cancer, I believe they are the reason I have survived all of the chemotherapy and radiation. I am now celebrating eleven years of being cancer free. I hope that someday we can all drop our egos and work together.

About two years ago I was involved in a car accident that left me with two large hematomas in my brain that required brain surgery. I know what it is to live with a disability, but in a body that can adapt. I believe that this is the key for someone to get their life back.

I hope the information that I have learned throughout my years in practice and have listed in this book can help people to understand what their body may be trying to tell them. Hopefully, they can then seek out the help that they need to regain the control and adaptability in their life, or in other words "Get Their Life Back"! I encourage all practitioners to investigate the underlying "triggers" I have listed here when they are working with any organ or glandular dysfunction. They may not be apparent but can be very influential and even the key in some circumstances to relieving the stress on that organ or gland. I hope the dimension work also helps you to discover any hidden or deeper issues that may not be apparent but will help you give your patients the relief they deserve.

I am very grateful if any of the information in this book will give you, the practitioner and/or the patient, the insight and relief you deserve.

I welcome all comments and questions at **www.STORKANCHIROPRACTIC.COM.**

Thank you!

DR. Gary

References

Adrenal Fatigue, (the 21st Century Stress Syndrome)   James L. Wilson ND, DC, PhD, Smart Publishing, Petaluma, CA   2001

Anatomy, (A Regional Atlas of the Human Body)   Carmine D. Clemente, Lea & Febiger, Philadelphia, PA, 1975

Applied Kinesiology, (The Advanced Approach in Chiropractic) David S. Walther DC   Systems DC, Pueblo, CO   CR1976 (100 hour course)

Biology of Belief, Bruce Lipton PhD,   Mountain of Love/Elite Books, Santa Ros, CA, 2005

Contact Reflex Analysis, (weekend course)   D.A. Versendaal DC, Holland, MI,   1976 & 1991

The Divine Matrix, Gregg Braden, Hay House Inc., Carlsbad, CA,   2007

Essentials of Skeletal Radiology, Volumes 1 & 2   Terry R. Yochum, Lindsay J. Rowe   Williams & Wilkins, Baltimore, MD   1987

Enzyme Nutrition, Dr. Edward Howell   Avery Publishing, Wayne, NJ 1985

Freedom from Fear Forever, (acupower)   James V. Durlacher DC   VanNess Publishing, Mesa, AZ 1995

Food Enzymes for Health Longevity, Dr. Edward Howell   Lotus Press, Twin Lakes, WI 1994

Guess What Came to Dinner, (Parasites and Your Health)   Ann Louise Gittleman   Avery Publishing, Garden

City Park, NY 1993

Hyperspace, (A Scientific Odyssey through Parallel Universe, Time Warps, and the 10th Dimension)   Michio Kaku, Anchor Books, NY 1995

Iodine, (Why You Need It) David Brownstein MD, Medical Alternatives Press, West Bloomfield MI 2009

In Bad Taste, (The MSG Symptom Complex)   George R. Schwartz MD   Health Press, Santa Fe, NM 1999

Illustrated Manual of Neurological Reflexes, Signs, Tests and Orthopedic Signs, Tests, and Maneuvers   Dr. J. M. Mazion   Second Ed. Daniels Publishing, Orlando, FL 1980

Illustrated Physiology, McNought and Callander   Churchill Livingstone, Edinburgh, London 3rd edition 1975

Misdiagnosed, (The Adrenal Fatigue Link)   Steven M. Zodkoy DC, CNS, DACBN, DCBCN   Babypie Publishing, Waitsfield, VT 2014

Myofascial Pain and Dysfunction, (The Trigger Point Manual) Volumes 1 & 2   Janet G. Travell MD, David G. Simons MD   Williams & Wilkins Publishing, Baltimore, MD 1983

Medical Physiology, (9th edition) Guyton and Hall W.B. Saunders Co 1996

Overcoming Thyroid Disorders, (2nd edition) David Brownstein MD   Medical Alternative Press, West Bloomfield, MI 2008

Parallel Worlds, Michio Kaku   Anchor Books, New York, NY 2006

Radiology of Bone Diseases, (3rd edition)   George B. Greenfield MD,   J.B. Lippincott, Philadelphia, PA 1975

Stretching, Bob Anderson   Shelter Publishing 1980

The Secrety of Energy, Marcie Martinez BS, ChE, MS, M Sc   Natures Presence 2018

Trace Elements and Other Essential Nutrients   Dr. David L. Watts   Publisher, Dallas, TX 1995

Thyroid, (Guardian of Health)   Philip G. Young MD   Trafford Publishing, Victoria, BC 2002

Touch for Health, John Thie DC   DeVorss Publishing, Camarillo, CA 2009

Several Seminars with Biotics, Nutriwest, Systemic Formulas and Erchonia Corporations

The Stress of Life, (General Adaptive Syndrome)   Hans Selye MD   McGraw-Hill, New York, NY 1956

Total Body Modification: 2505 Anthem Village Dr, Suite E221, Henderson, NV 89052   (435) 652-4340
web site: www.totalbodymodification.com

Ergopathics Vials: email   vials@ergopathics. com
T: 1-888-959-6728

About the Author

Dr. Storkan began his journey into alternative health in 1973, after being trained in massage therapy in California. He then made a journey to the East Coast settling in Cape Cod, Massachusetts. At that time, he was working as a carpenter.

After an injury, he sought the help of a local chiropractor. During his session, the chiropractor did several muscle tests on him and corrected their dysfunction by rubbing several sore points. This so intrigued Dr. Storkan that he had to ask where this doctor had learned this technique. He was told about the Touch for Health Foundation in Pasadena, California.

The following year, Dr. Storkan returned to California and contacted the TFH Foundation in 1975. He enrolled in their instructor training program and became one of their instructors.

After teaching for several months, he was approached by another instructor who was the office manager of a very large chiropractic practice in northern California.

He saw this as an opportunity to develop his muscle testing skills in a therapeutic setting and therefore was hired to treat patients by resetting their muscles after a chiropractic adjustment. He also did some nutritional counseling with the patients.

He worked with this practice for about three years and during that time, witnessed some profound healing in patients precipitated by the chiropractic adjustments. He decided that he would like to pursue a degree in that profession.

Dr. Storkan did some research on many of the chiropractic schools that were available and decided on Logan College of Chiropractic in Baldwin, Missouri. He liked their approach and focus on both the sciences and philosophy of chiropractic, and the fact that they were one of the few chiropractic schools with national accreditation at the time.

This meant they could accept the GI bill for payment. After taking the prerequisite courses, he entered Logan College in 1979. During his time at Logan, he took several extracurricular courses and was certified in advanced x-ray interpretation, motion palpation, and several adjusting techniques trying to find the one with which he felt the most comfortable. He even took a semester off to restudy information that he felt was coming in too fast for him to completely absorb and understand.

During this time, he reread and studied his physiology and neurology textbooks and studied more nutrition. It was a very productive time for him. Dr. Storkan graduated from Logan College of Chiropractic in the spring of 1983.

Dr. Storkan has pursued his thirst for knowledge after graduating from Logan with several seminars each year including the entire Diplomate of Chiropractic Orthopedics course.

He has also taken an extensive Functional Medicine course with Dr. Lundell, and several modules of the Total Body Modification technique with the master and founder, Dr. Victor Frank. He is now pursuing training and information in the use of cold lasers through the Erchonia Corporation.

Dr. Storkan has also gained much valuable knowledge from his patients that he has had the pleasure of working with for the last 35 years.

Visit the Author website at **storkanchiropractic.com**

www.ingramcontent.com/pod-product-compliance
Lightning Source LLC
Chambersburg PA
CBHW030900170426
43193CB00009BA/682